THE QUEEN'S DIAMOND
JUBILEE GALLERIES
WESTMINSTER ABBEY

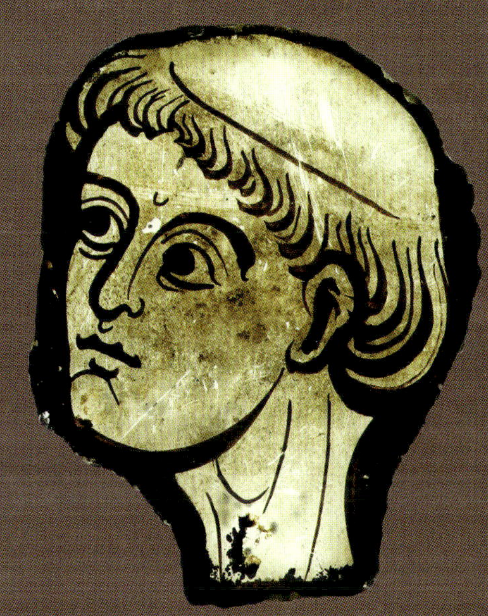

Edited by Susan Jenkins and Tony Trowles
Assisted by Julia Snape
Contributors Matthew Payne and Warwick Rodwell

SCALA

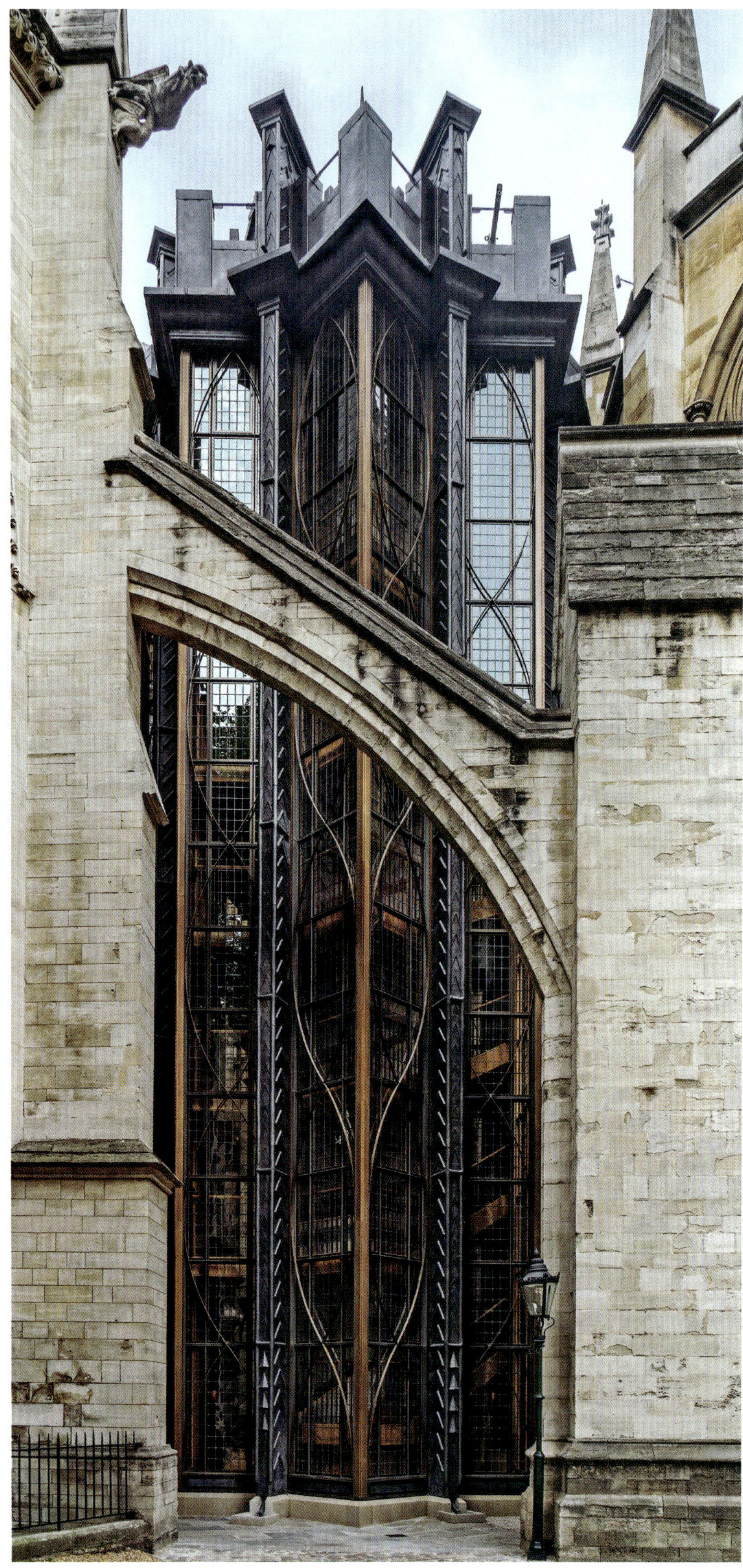

This edition © Scala Arts & Heritage Publishers
Ltd, 2023
Text © Westminster Abbey Enterprises Ltd
Photography © The Dean and Chapter
of Westminster except as listed below
p.15 (bottom) Stuart Harrison
p.16 (right) Paul Binski (shrine fragment)
p.20 (top right) Bodleian Library,
University of Oxford
p.39 Press Association
p.42 Hulton Royals Collection / Getty Images

First published in 2018 by
Scala Arts & Heritage Publishers Ltd
305 Access House
141–157 Acre Lane
London SW2 5UA
www.scalapublishers.com

Reprinted 2023

ISBN 978 1 78551 131 8

Edited by Jessica Hodge
Designed by Raymonde Watkins
Printed and bound in Turkey

10 9 8 7 6 5 4 3

Note
Dates for monarchs are regnal dates

The editors wish to thank the following
Lucy Ackland, Krista Blessley, Ian Bristow,
Marian Campbell, Stuart Frost, Richard
Gem, Philippa Glanville, John Goodall,
Diana Heath, Gordon Higgott, Maurice
Howard, Edward Impey, Nigel Israel,
Kathryn Jones, Michael Kauffmann,
Richard Marks, John McNeill, Liz Miller,
David Mitchell, Lisa Monnas, Peta Motture,
Tom O'Keeffe, Tony Platt, Christine Reynolds,
Warwick Rodwell, Tim Schroder, Leonie
Seliger, Vanessa Simeoni, Sir Roy Strong,
Tim Tatton-Brown, Alan Williams

*The Weston Tower designed by
Ptolemy Dean Architects*

CONTENTS

Foreword   4
The Very Reverend Dr David Hoyle, MBE
Dean of Westminster

Introduction   6

1   **Building Westminster Abbey**   10

2   **Worship and Daily Life**   24

3   **Westminster Abbey and the Monarchy**   36

4   **The Abbey and National Memory**   50

Donor Acknowledgements   64

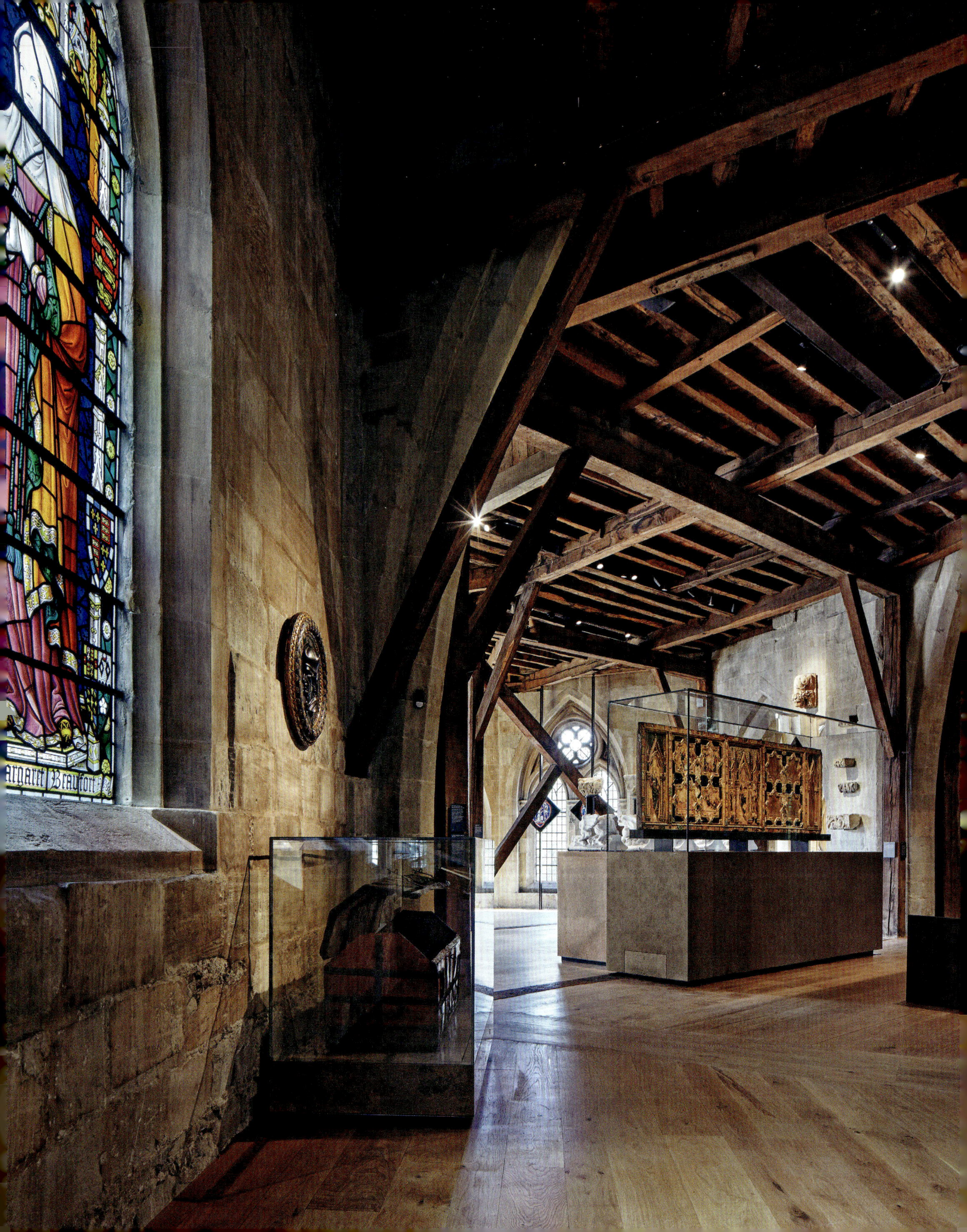

FOREWORD

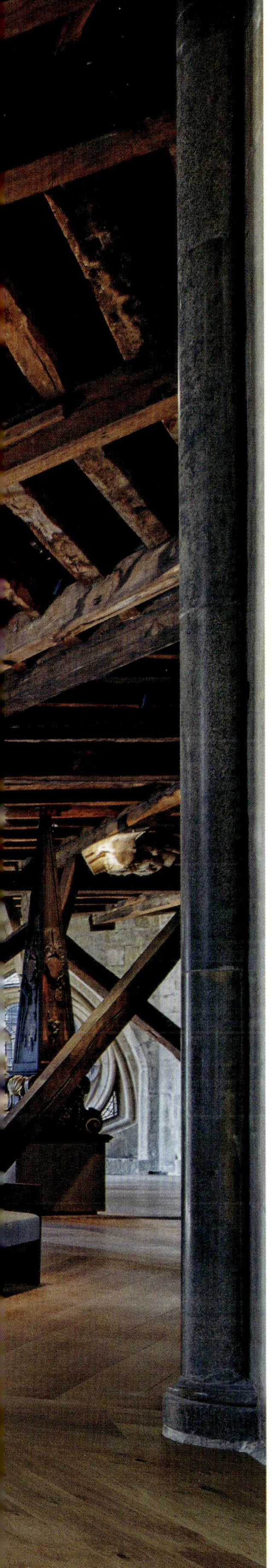

High above the floor of the Abbey, the Galleries are a breathtaking space, flooded with light. They have served as a vantage point to witness coronations and as storage for items we thought we might need one day. In 2012 the decision was taken to adapt the space to tell the story of the Abbey and offer our visitors the chance to see great treasures that are part of a long, rich past. They opened in 2018.

A visit to the Galleries is a marvellous experience and in planning the exhibition we wanted to honour the space as well as the objects within it. You will find here reminders that the Abbey has been a theatre for monarchy in life and death. You will find here too a little of the sustained rhythm of prayer and praise that has been the steady pulse of a building that keeps faith at the heart of the nation.

The Very Reverend Dr David Hoyle, MBE, Dean of Westminster

Sunbeams and shadows in the Galleries

INTRODUCTION

ESTMINSTER ABBEY IS IN THE UNUSUAL, but fortunate, position of having a high-level tribune gallery, the triforium, that runs all the way round the church as far as the western towers. It sits behind the inner wall of the upper ambulatory, looking down on the sanctuary and the Shrine of St Edward the Confessor, and dates from the reign of Henry III (1216–72). The Queen's Diamond Jubilee Galleries have been created in the eastern part of the triforium.

It was common for large Anglo-Saxon and Norman churches to have high-level galleries, and suites of chapels on upper floors as well as at ground level. This practice continued into the thirteenth century, falling out of fashion after a few decades, but the upper storey was an integral part of the design of Henry III's new abbey and was constructed in the 1250s. The chapels were never finished internally, nor were they decorated or brought into use, and for centuries they stood as huge empty spaces, gradually filling up with lumber.

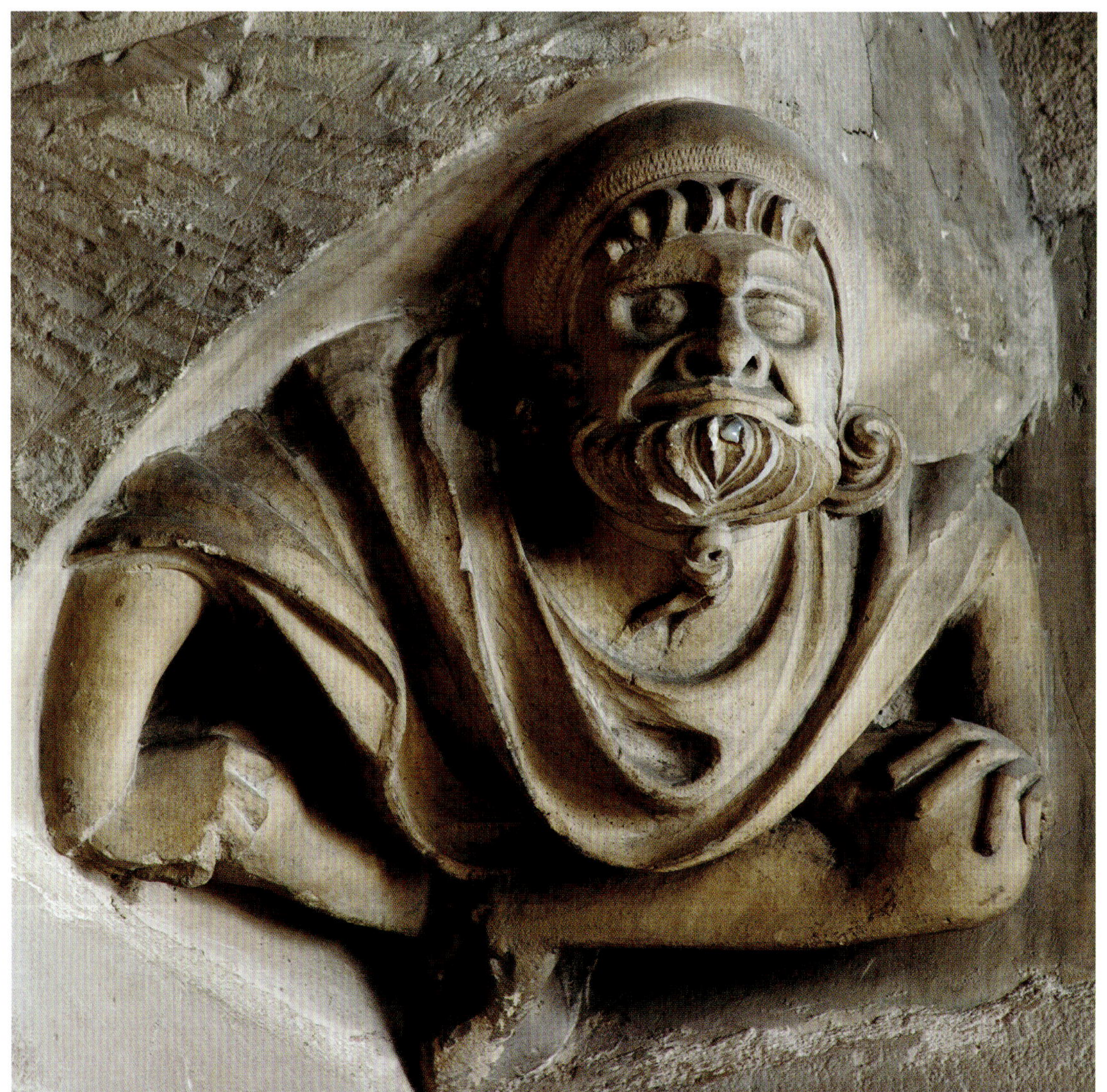

Caen stone corbel of a craftsman wearing a cap, about 1250–55

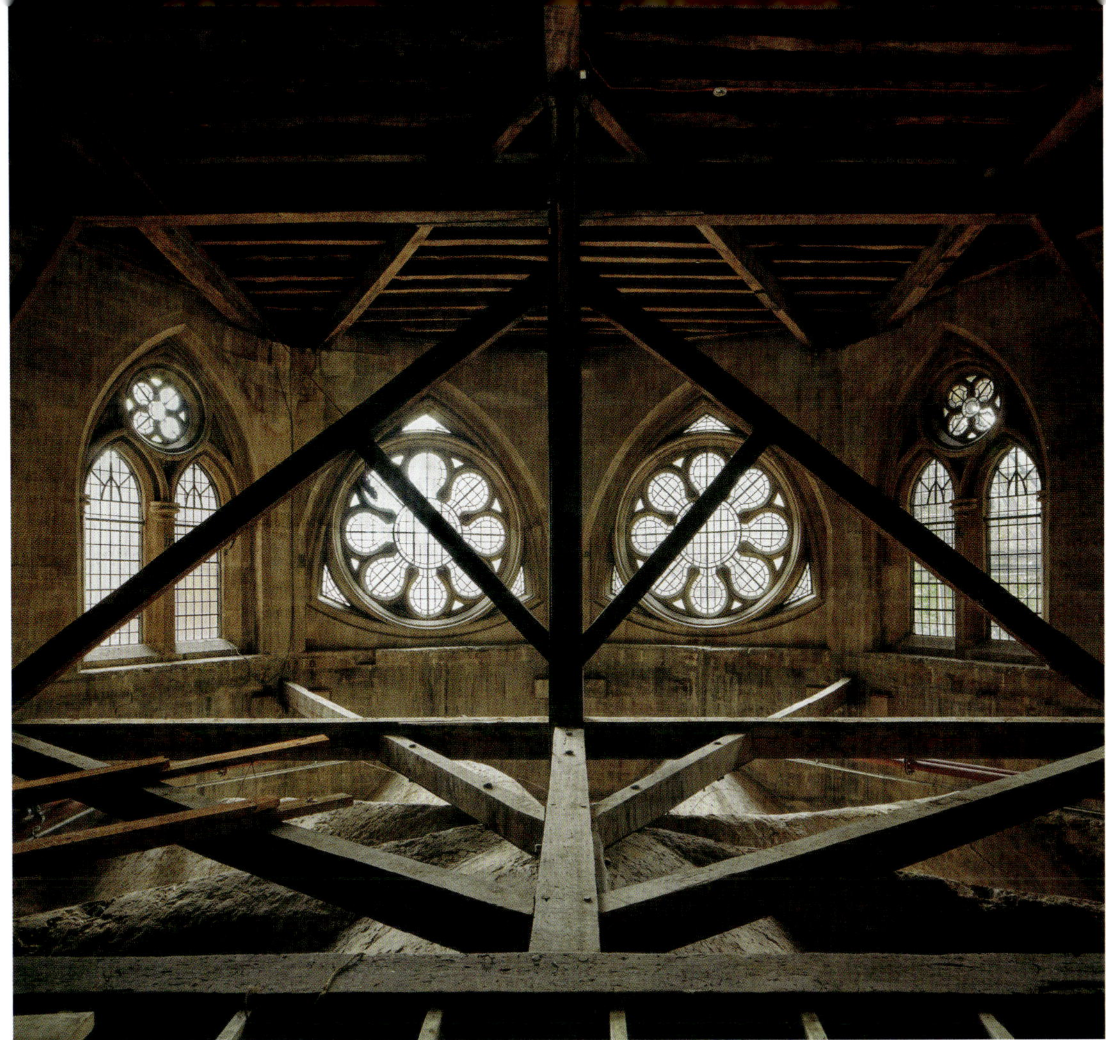

The tops of the stone vaults exposed before laying the new oak floor in the triforium

It was originally intended that the architecture within the triforium gallery and chapels would be as ornate as that in the rest of the church, with fine mouldings, polished Purbeck marble shafts, beautifully carved human and grotesque stone heads, and painted decoration everywhere. The Caen stone corbels supporting the gallery roof timbers include carved heads that rank amongst the finest surviving thirteenth-century English sculpture. Traces of coloured pigments remain on these but, surprisingly, there are no traces of paint on the bare stone walls and window mouldings, which suggests that the decorative scheme may never have been fully finished.

Today the triforium has flat lead roofs, but in the original design there would probably have been high-pointed octagonal roofs over the chapels, similar to those still seen on French cathedrals such as Amiens. The triforium roofs were reconstructed and flattened in the fifteenth century, but by 1699 they were falling into decay and the architect Sir Christopher Wren began a major overhaul of the roofs, reconstructing them in their present form. He inserted the massive oak supporting frames and braces, which in turn are carried by a complex timber framework beneath the floors.

Wren was also responsible for installing the first timber flooring throughout the triforium. It is likely that in the thirteenth century the gallery and chapels were intended to be paved with decorative ceramic tiles, but these were never laid. Consequently, the uneven upper surfaces of the stone vaults that cover the ambulatory and chapels at ground level would have been exposed to view. It would have been impossible to walk about in the triforium before Wren constructed the timber floors as the undulations of the tops of the vaults were so great, forming craters more than 1.5 metres deep. Once a flat timber floor had been inserted, the triforium became a usable

space, not only for storage but also as a viewing
gallery for great services, such as coronations
and royal funerals, which took place in the body
of the Abbey below. Numerals were painted
on the walls to identify the viewing bays, and
appropriately numbered tickets were issued to
participants. Four such tickets for Queen Anne's
coronation, on 23 April 1702, were found here.

Before the new oak floor was laid in 2016,
the dirt and rubbish that had accumulated over
the centuries in the vault pockets was cleaned
out. More than 4,000 sacks were filled and sorted
by archaeologists, who recovered an astonishing
array of historic artefacts spanning 750 years.
These included 30,000 pieces of window glass,
some beautifully decorated, and an assortment
of stone fragments, metal objects, pottery, tools,
shoes, documents, playing cards, tobacco packets
and other debris left behind by workmen and
people who had watched services from the gallery.

Access to the triforium was via two spiral
stone staircases in the corners of the north and
south transepts. The first proposal that visitors
to the Abbey should be allowed to ascend these
to enjoy the spectacular views was made in 1842,
but no action was taken. Instead, in the later
nineteenth century, historic artefacts began to be
deposited in the triforium, and in 1988 these were
arranged as a display, named the Lapidarium,
which scholars could view by appointment.

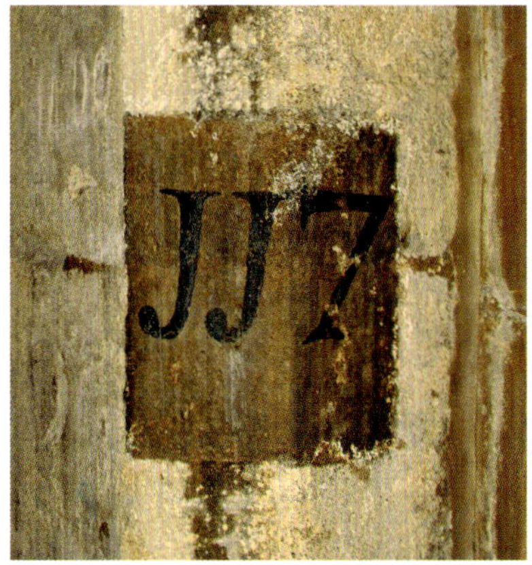

*Right: A number
(117) probably
painted by Wren's
craftsmen to identify
the bay*

*Below: Ceremonial
helmets associated
with the Order of
the Bath displayed in
the triforium in 1896*

*Bottom: Floorplan
showing the galleries
in the east triforium*

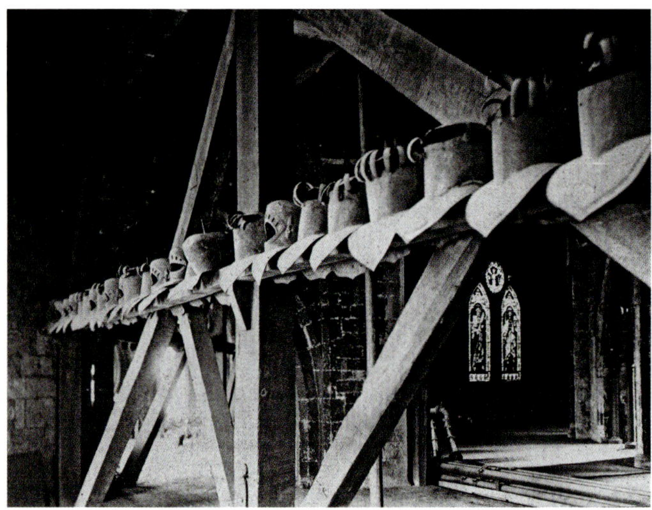

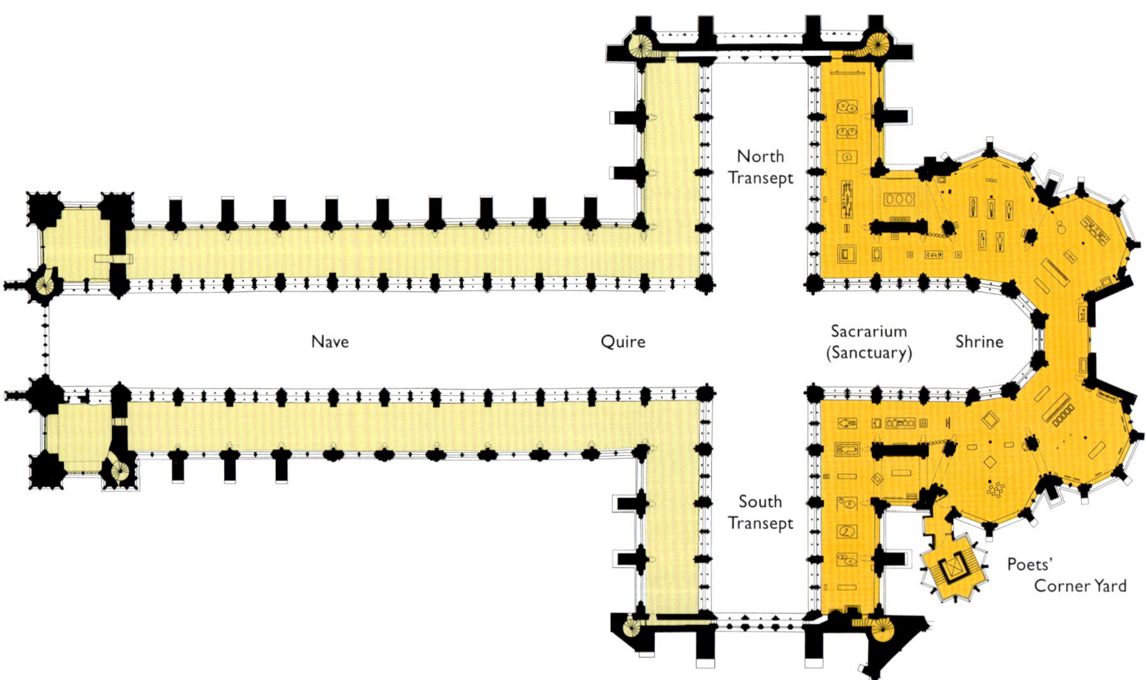

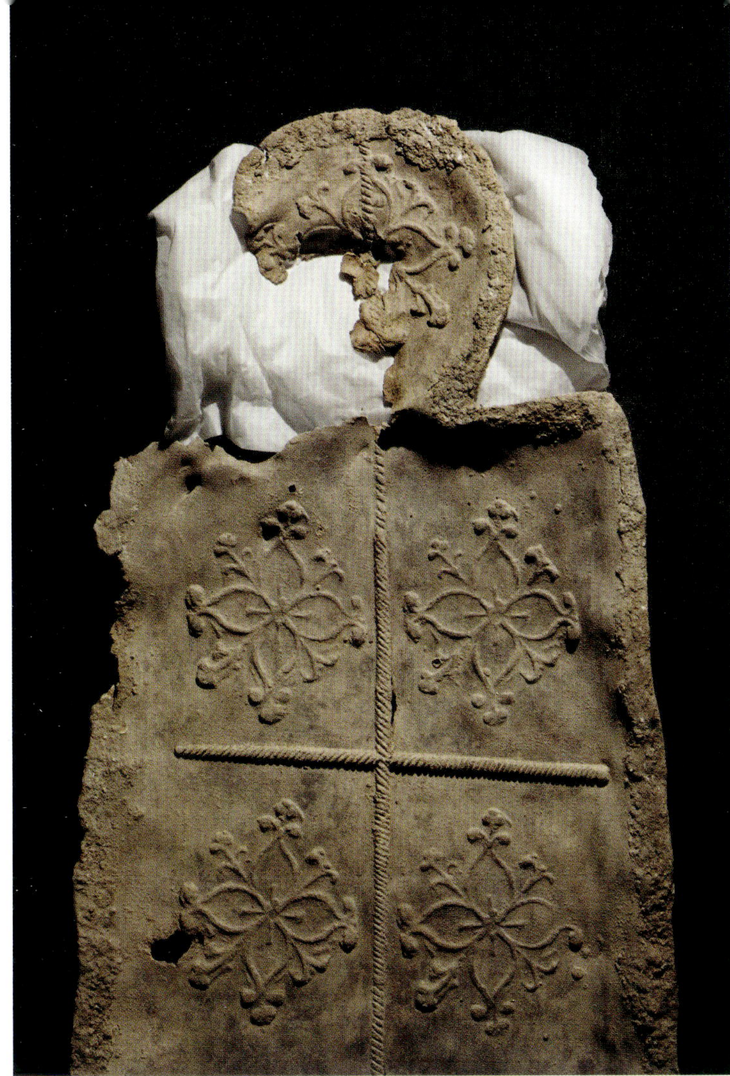

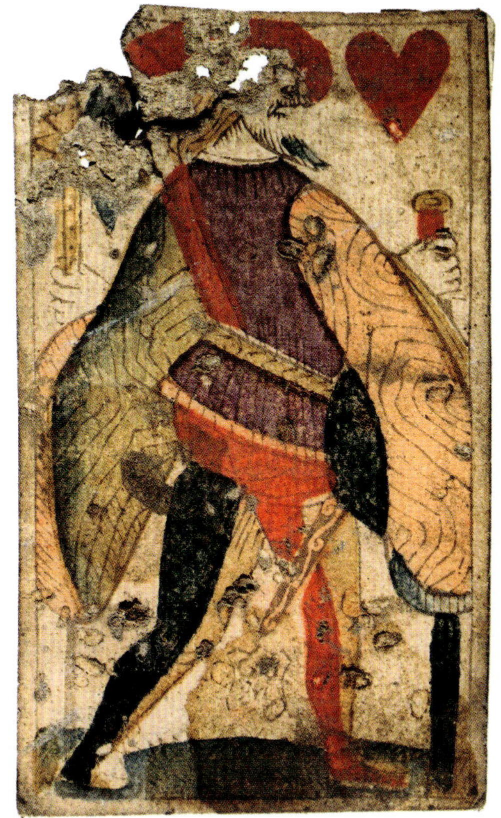

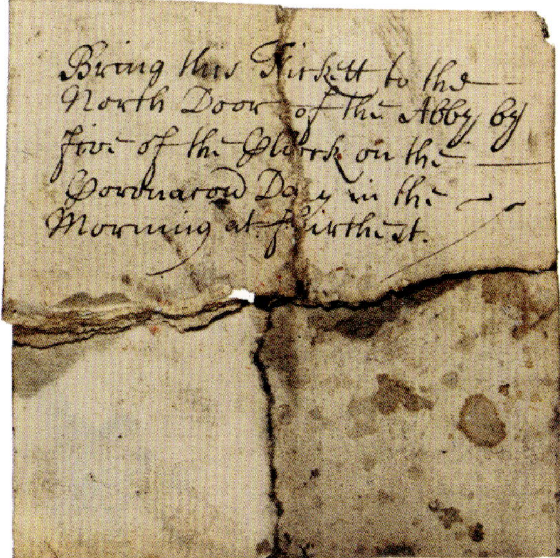

Above: The head end of a fifteenth-century decorated lead coffin excavated in Poets' Corner Yard in 2015

Right: Items discovered during cleaning of the vault pockets: a seventeenth-century playing card and a hand-written ticket for Queen Anne's coronation in 1702

The medieval staircases are not suitable for large numbers of visitors today and so a new access tower, designed by Surveyor of the Fabric Ptolemy Dean, has been constructed alongside the south transept, in a small outside area known as Poets' Corner Yard. Before the tower was constructed, full archaeological excavation of the site took place, revealing medieval foundations and graves from the Anglo-Saxon period onwards. The most important burials were in limestone and lead coffins, and one of the latter was outstanding. At one end of the coffin, the lead was carefully shaped to follow the outline of the head and shoulders of the body; this very rare coffin shape, known as 'anthropoid', is mostly associated with royal and noble burials. The lid is uniquely decorated with a long cross and a series of floriated motifs, all cast in lead. The design suggests a fifteenth-century date, but the identity of the person remains unknown.

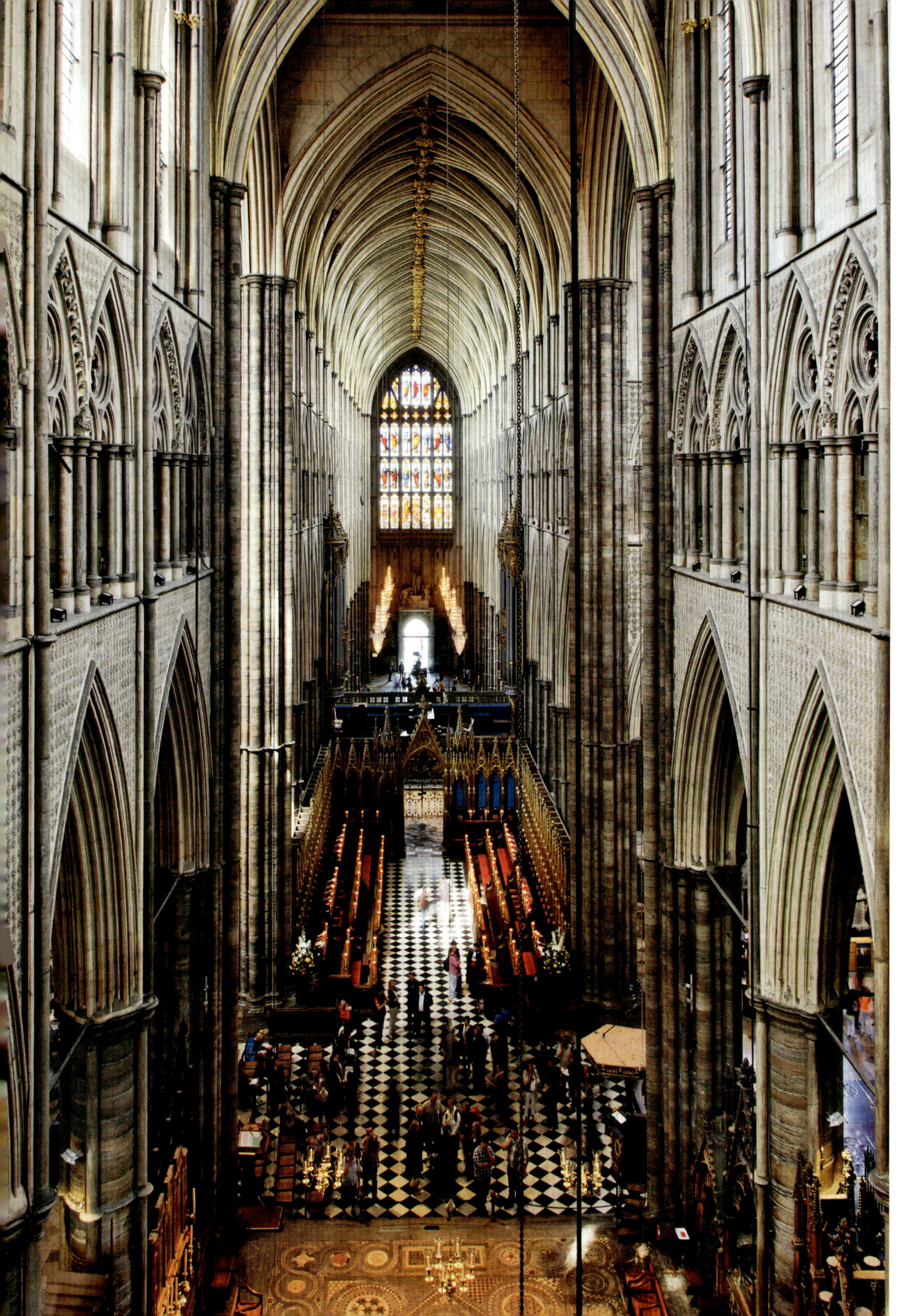

1 BUILDING WESTMINSTER ABBEY

WESTMINSTER ABBEY WAS founded in the Anglo-Saxon period as a 'minster' (mother church) to the west of London, dedicated to St Peter. It was probably built on the sandy Isle of Thorns or Thorney, where the River Tyburn met the Thames. A forged twelfth-century document purporting to date from AD 785 records a grant of land by the Mercian king Offa 'to St Peter and the needy people of God in Thorney in the terrible place which is called at Westminster'. The first certain evidence for the existence of the Abbey, however, is the arrival of the reforming cleric Dunstan in around AD 958–61, accompanied by 12 monks. With a grant of land and money from King Edgar, Dunstan refounded the existing minster as a Benedictine abbey; his church does not survive, but he was made a saint in AD 1029 in honour of his piety.

The earliest building on the Abbey site of which traces remain was the church begun in about AD 1050 by the Anglo-Saxon king Edward. The king decided to build a new palace next to his church. The Bayeux Tapestry shows this church with a central tower, which by now housed about 80 monks. The Abbey was consecrated on 28 December 1065, shortly before Edward's death on 5 January 1066. A cult of devotion to Edward developed, particularly after he was made a saint in 1161 and given the title 'Confessor', confirming that he had lived a model Christian life. St Edward the Confessor's body found its final resting place in the Abbey in 1269, when it was 'translated' by Henry III to a new shrine in his chapel to the east of the High Altar, where it still lies.

Henry III (1216–72) came to the throne aged nine and was to become one of the Abbey's most important patrons. He was devoted to the cult of St Edward the Confessor, his patron saint. His first coronation took place at Gloucester Abbey (now Cathedral), but he insisted on being crowned for a second time at Westminster Abbey on 17 May 1220. From 1245 Henry personally paid to rebuild the Abbey, employing master masons Henry of Reyns, John of Gloucester and Robert of Beverley, who also helped extend his nearby palace at Westminster. The work included demolishing the eastern part of St Edward the Confessor's church to make way for a new church and chapter house. Henry also commissioned a new high altar with a magnificent altarpiece (the Westminster Retable) and two marble 'Cosmati' pavements made by Italian craftsmen. These works were completed by 1269, when the body of St Edward was installed in its new position in the Shrine of St Edward the Confessor to the east. By the time of Henry III's death, the east end, transepts and five bays of the nave were completed. Henry was buried in the Abbey in 1272, and his body moved to a monumental Cosmati tomb in St Edward the Confessor's Chapel in 1290.

Henry III did not complete the rebuilding of Westminster Abbey; the east end of his new church remained attached to the nave of St Edward the Confessor's church. Life was further disrupted for the monks in 1298, when a fire damaged the cloisters where they spent much of their time. Rebuilding and reroofing the cloister buildings ensured that the monks' refectory (on the south) and dormitory (on the east) were soon repaired. Building work on the nave resumed under Richard II (1377–99), overseen by Abbot Nicholas Litlyngton, and continued into the reign of Henry VIII (1509–47). Several new monastic buildings were erected during Richard's lifetime, including the abbot's house in 1372 (now the Deanery) and the cellarer's range (south-west of the cloister), which included a brewhouse, bakehouse and granary. Henry V, who was buried in the Abbey on 7 November 1422, paid for the construction of the chantry chapel that stands over his tomb east of the shrine, which was completed in the 1440s.

View of the Abbey from the triforium

THE TUDORS AND STUARTS

In 1503 the first Tudor king, Henry VII, commissioned a new Lady Chapel, replacing the chapel constructed for Henry III, to offer prayers for his soul and provide a burial place for himself and his family. By the time of his death in 1509, it had cost him over £14,000. The architecture and design of the distinctive fan-vaulted ceiling is attributed to masons Robert Janyns or Robert and William Vertue. Originally, Henry VII had planned to bury his uncle Henry VI there but he failed to persuade the pope to canonise Henry, who was buried elsewhere. Instead, Henry VII himself and his wife Elizabeth of York were buried at the east end of the Lady Chapel. Their impressive tomb was made by Florentine sculptor Pietro Torrigiano and completed in 1518 at a cost of £1,500. The chapel was consecrated in 1516.

The next 200 years saw little building work at the Abbey. The Benedictine monastery was dissolved in January 1540, following Henry VIII's reformation of the English Church, by which time it had only 24 monks. Despite a brief revival under Mary I, it was finally abolished by her half-sister, Elizabeth I (1558–1603). The new queen established instead the Collegiate Church of St Peter, Westminster, by charter of 21 May 1560.

When Sir Christopher Wren was appointed the Surveyor of the Fabric in 1698, the Abbey was beginning to show its age. Wren oversaw an extensive repair programme, including reroofing parts of the Abbey. He also designed a new tower and spire to stand over the crossing, which were never built. His successor as surveyor, Nicholas Hawksmoor, designed the west towers, which were completed during the surveyorship of John James in 1745.

LATER WORKS

More recently, surveyors Edward Blore, Sir George Gilbert Scott and their successors have undertaken restoration work both outside and inside the Abbey. In 1821, the large altarpiece from Whitehall Palace chapel, designed by Wren, was removed from the Abbey's High Altar in preparation for the coronation of George IV. In the 1840s, Blore replaced the medieval choir stalls with new seating. Scott was an active surveyor, installing a new High Altar, 1867–73, and restoring the

chapter house. Restoration work on the north transept and portal was completed by Scott's successors, John Loughborough Pearson and John Thomas Micklethwaite.

On the night of 10 May 1941, the Abbey sustained multiple direct hits from German incendiary bombs, one of which burnt out the lantern tower over the crossing, which was repaired by the surveyor Stephen Dykes Bower. A programme of cleaning the Abbey exterior and the Lady Chapel interior was completed in the 1990s, when the Lady Chapel and the west front were restored and new figures of Christian martyrs and virtues were installed above and beside the Great West Door.

The Queen's Diamond Jubilee Galleries, designed by MUMA (McInnes Usher McKnight Architects) in the triforium space, opened in 2018, supported by a lift tower, the Weston Tower, which was designed by Surveyor of the Fabric Ptolemy Dean. These are the first additions to the fabric of the Abbey since 1745 and sustain the tradition of careful development at Westminster Abbey over the centuries.

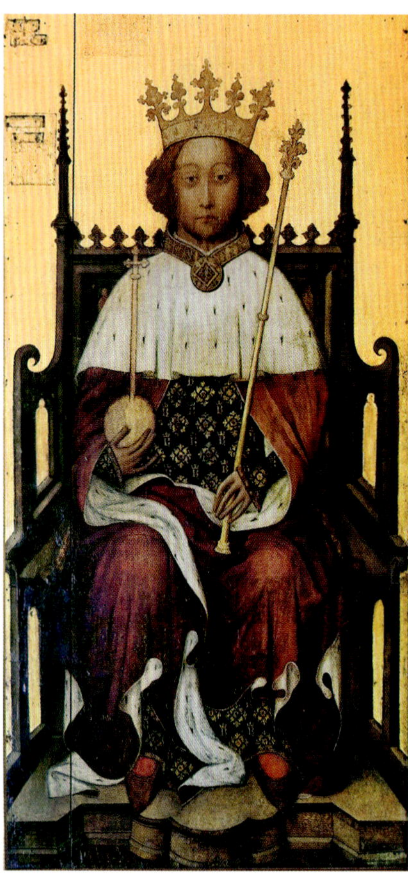

Left: Portrait of Richard II, about 1398, at the west end of the nave

Opposite: Tomb effigies of Henry VII and Elizabeth of York by Pietro Torrigiano

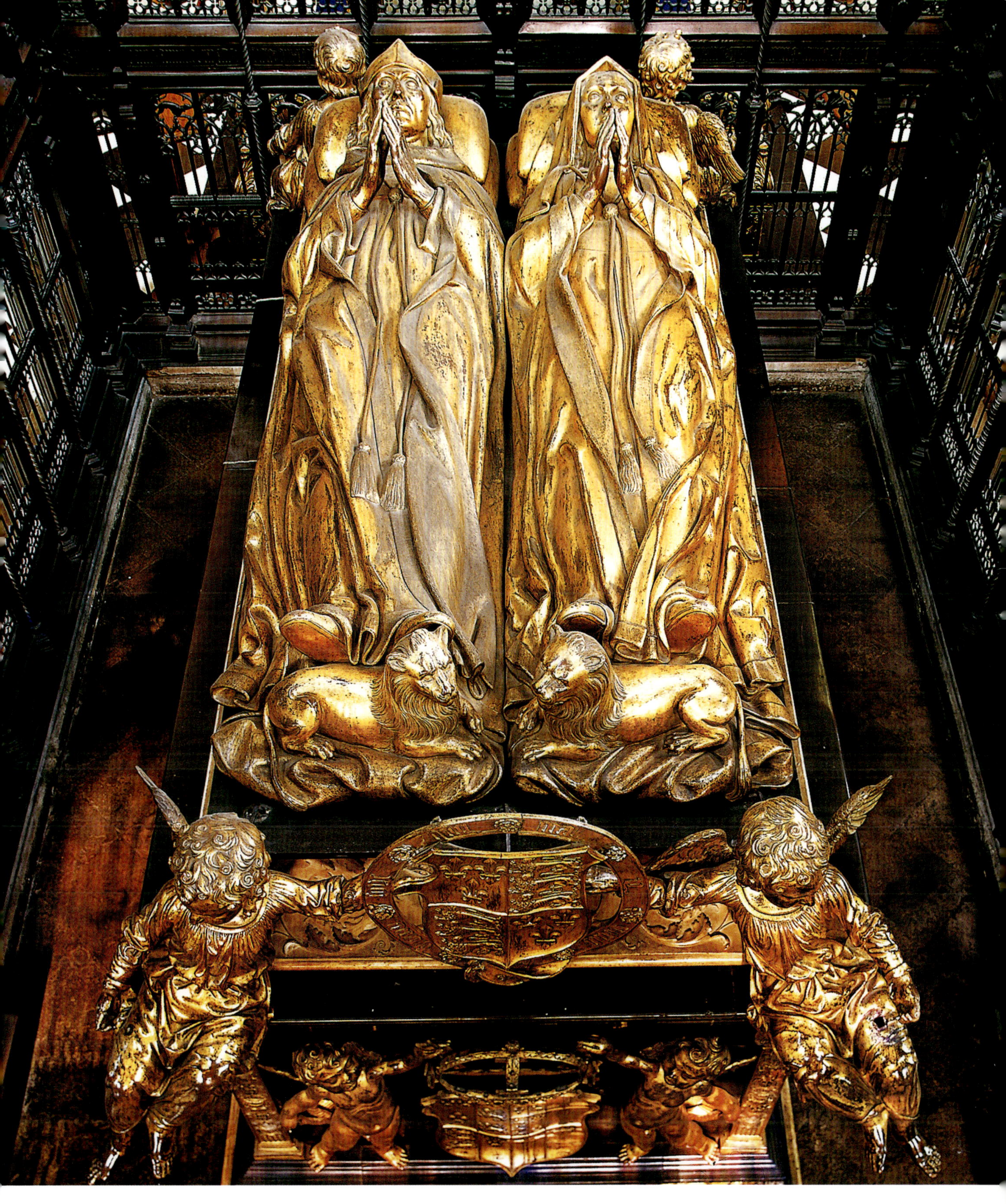

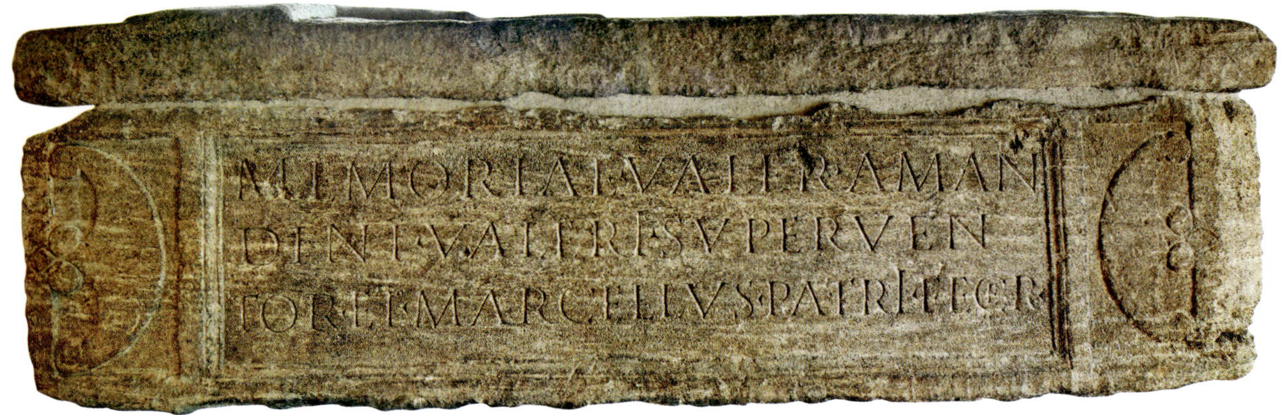

1 Roman Sarcophagus, about AD 300–400

Roman pottery has been found on the site of Westminster Abbey, suggesting a minor settlement here. This Roman sarcophagus, made from Taynton oolitic limestone, was dug up on the Abbey's North Green in 1869 and probably came originally from a mausoleum in one of the city's Roman cemeteries. It is one of only three or four Roman inscribed stone coffins excavated in London and was used for two burials – a Roman one in about AD 300–400 and a Saxon one in about AD 900–1000. The first burial was that of Valerius Amandinus, who was probably a well-off army officer. The stonework is boldly cut on one side with fine lettering which reads: 'MEMORIAE. VALER. AMANDINI VALERI. SUPERVENTOR. ET. MARCELLUS. PATRI. FECER' (in memory of Valerius Amandinus, the Valerii, Superventor and Marcellus, made this for their father.) There are two shield-like carved Roman ornaments ('*peltae*') at each corner. The splayed Latin cross carved in low relief on the coffin lid was added when the coffin was re-used for an unidentified occupant, possibly an Anglo-Saxon nobleman or a monk.

When the sarcophagus was discovered, the lid was removed and the skeleton examined by a doctor, who reported that it was that of a powerfully built man, below middle age. In 1873 the Surveyor of the Fabric, Sir George Gilbert Scott, mistakenly reported that the coffin was empty. During recent conservation work, however, a skeleton was confirmed to be inside. Analysis shows that it dates from approximately AD 1000, and is probably the skeleton of the sarcophagus's second, Anglo-Saxon, occupant.

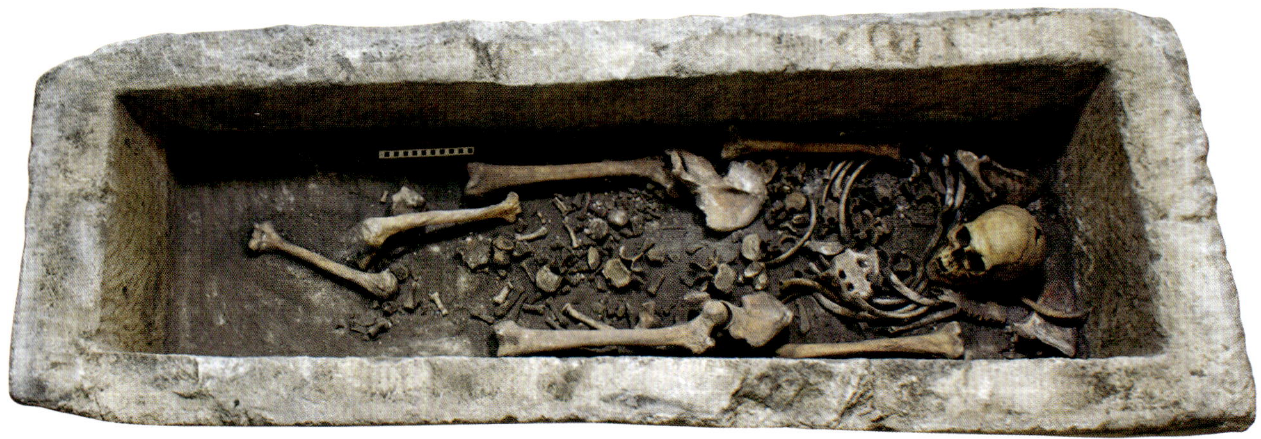

2 Column Capital from St Edward the Confessor's cloister, about 1100

The cloister was an active part of the monastery, where the monks spent their time reading, studying and occasionally playing games like 'nine holes'. The original cloister built by St Edward the Confessor was probably damaged by fire in 1298 and this capital, from the top of a column in the cloister arcade, is among the few to survive from the earlier period. It dates from about 1100; each of its faces shows a different scene from the Old Testament biblical story of the Judgement of Solomon on two women who both claim to be the mother of the same child. On one face (above right) both women plead their case before King Solomon; on another (below right) there is public acclaim at the king's judgement in ordering that the child be divided with the sword. The monks' dormitory was on the east side of the cloister, with their refectory and latrine (reredorter) on the south side.

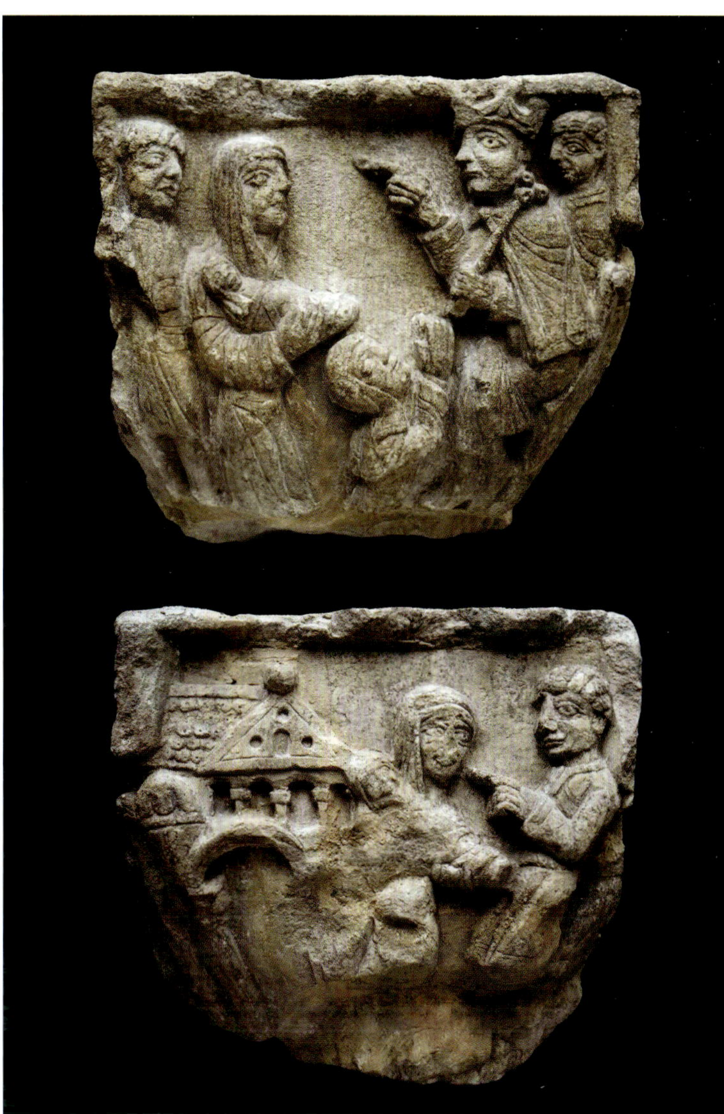

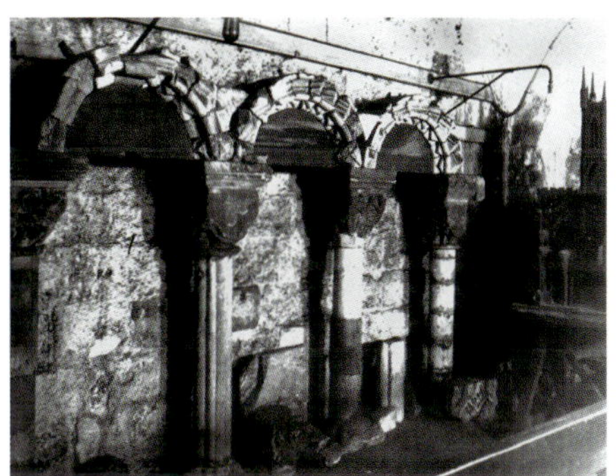

Left: A section of the cloister arcade reconstructed by W.R. Lethaby in the 1920s

Below: Reconstruction of a section of the cloister arcade in about 1150, drawn by Stuart Harrison

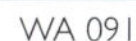
WA 0912

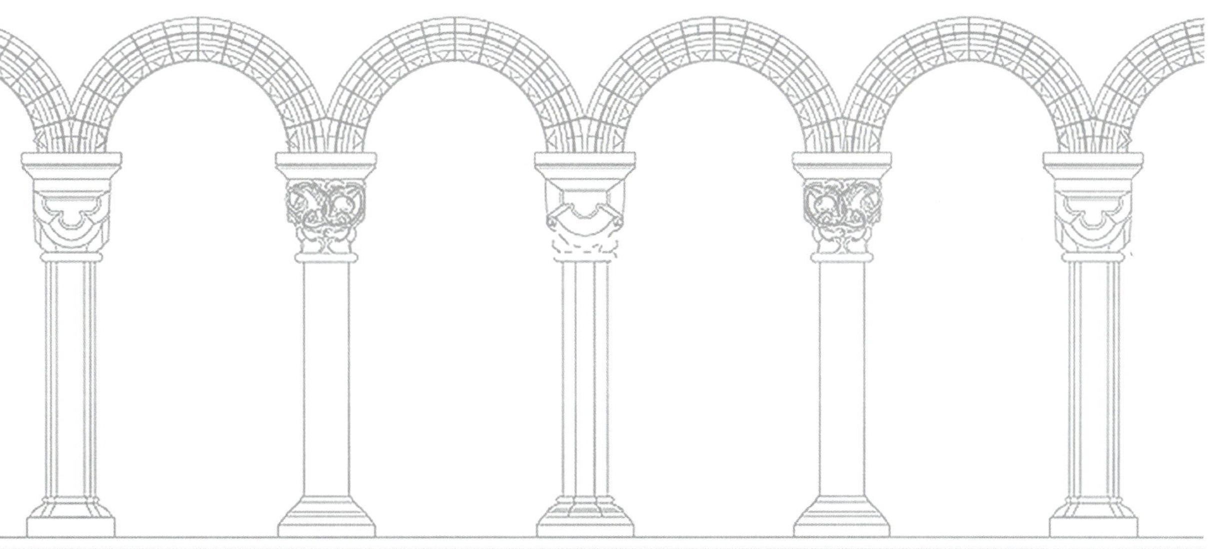

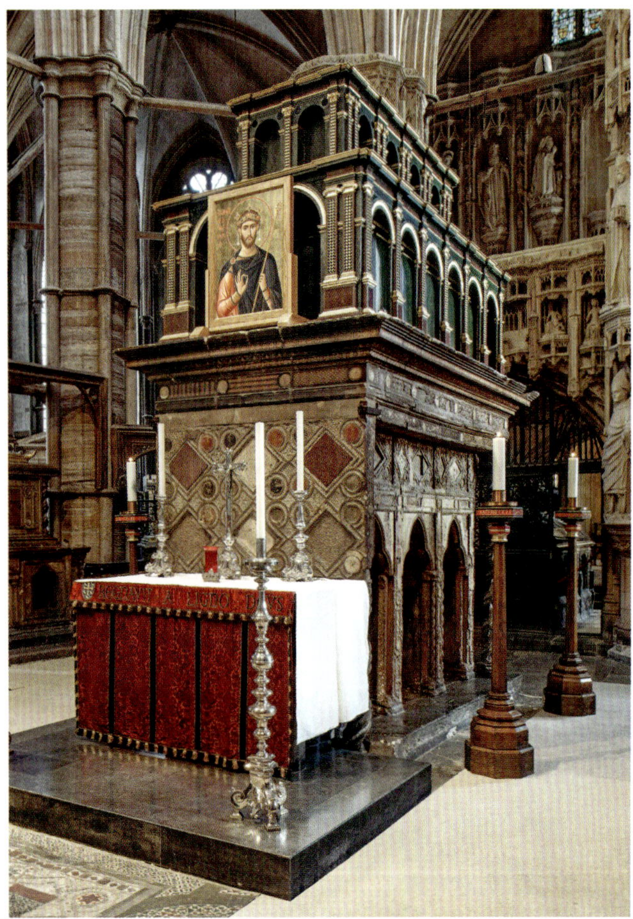

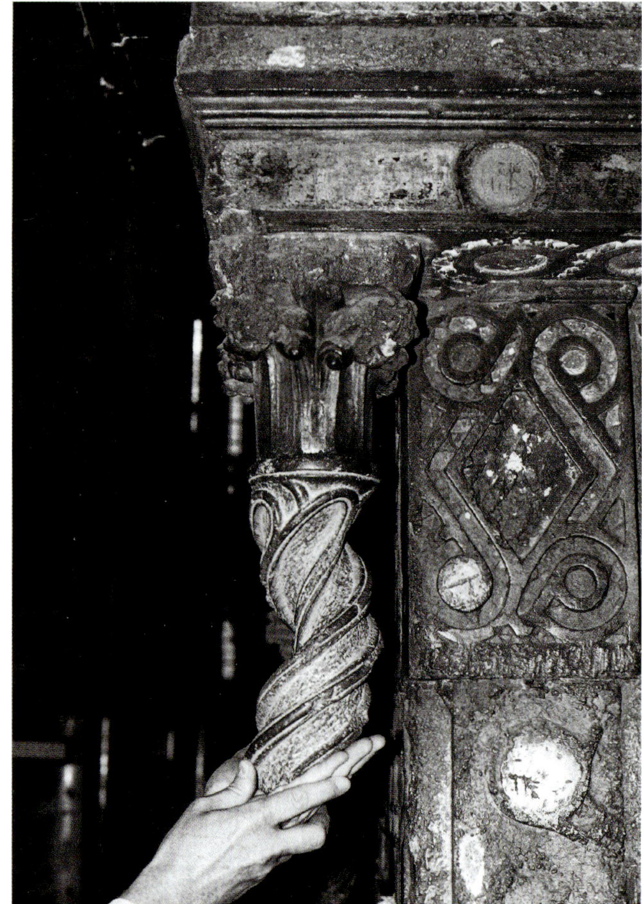

3 Purbeck marble colonnette from Shrine base of St Edward the Confessor, 1269

This twisted Purbeck marble colonnette became detached from the north-east corner of the Shrine of St Edward the Confessor, probably after it was dismantled in the 1540s. The shrine was originally decorated with coloured stones and glass inlays in a type of work known as Cosmati, after the Italian craftsmen who perfected the technique. The marble base of the shrine was made by 'Peter, citizen of Rome', who inscribed his name on it. Commissioned by Henry III, the shrine contains St Edward's body, which was moved here in 1269, and stands in its own chapel behind the High Altar, at the heart of Westminster Abbey.

Henry III is buried a few feet to the north and both kings are surrounded by other monarchs, including Edward I, Edward III and Richard II. Now hidden from public view, the shrine could originally be seen from the sacrarium (sanctuary) and the High Altar, which were decorated with inlaid pavements of Cosmati work.

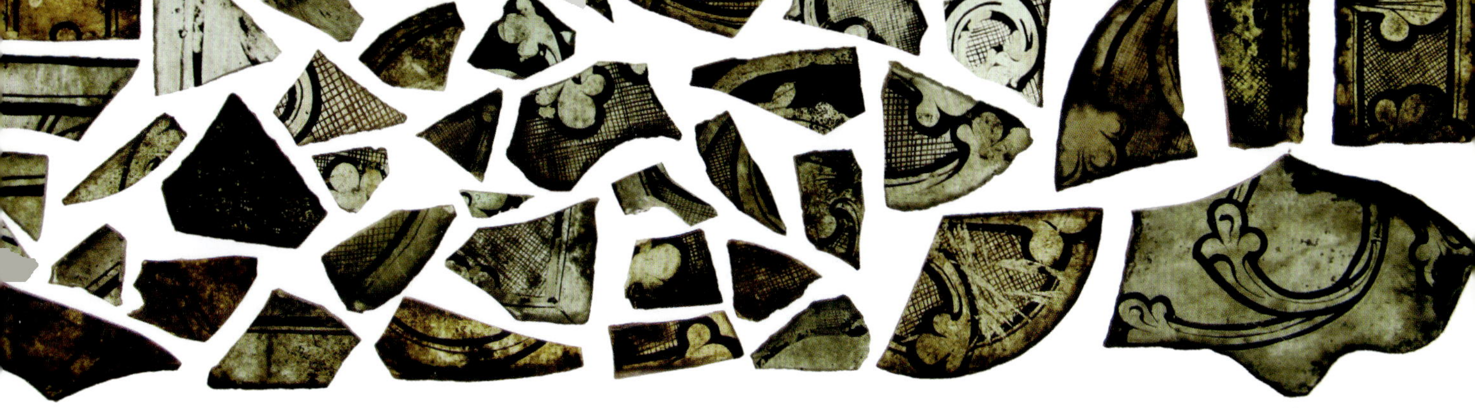

4 Stained Glass, 1250–1500

The fragments of medieval glass on display in the gallery
are important survivals from Henry III's new church. Glass
was expensive (coloured glass was twice the price of white
glass) and these panels may have been re-used in different
locations. Windows of grisaille glass (painting in black
line on colourless glass, using floral or leaf designs, cross-
hatching and pieces of coloured glass) were commonly
found in medieval churches; colourless panels allowed
more light into church interiors. In 1253 the building
accounts show that Westminster Abbey bought
coloured and white glass from Lawrence the Glazier
to make grisaille windows.

During restoration work in preparation for the
opening of The Queen's Diamond Jubilee Galleries,
30,000 small fragments of glass dating from between
1250 and 1500 were found under the floor of the triforium.
Examined altogether, this previously undiscovered cache
of glass sheds new light on the Abbey's glazing. It included
painted figurative pieces, inscriptions, heraldry and grisaille.
It may have resulted from the extensive reglazing in the
Abbey and the building works in the triforium undertaken
by Sir Christopher Wren from about 1700. Some of these
pieces have been re-used in windows that glaze the bridge
between the Weston Tower lift and the Galleries.

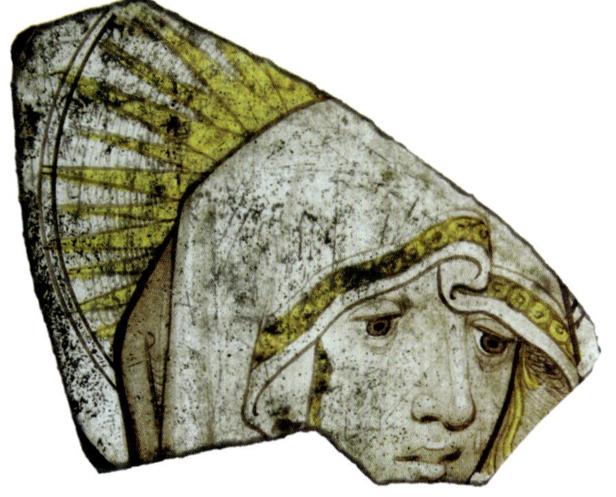

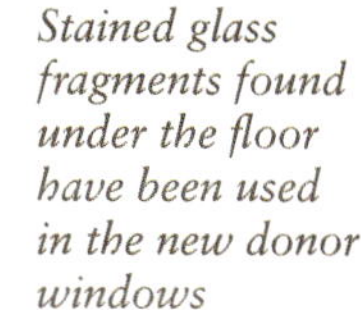

*Stained glass
fragments found
under the floor
have been used
in the new donor
windows*

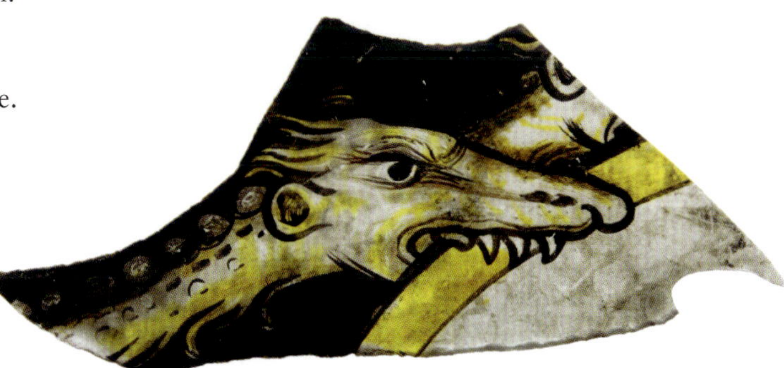

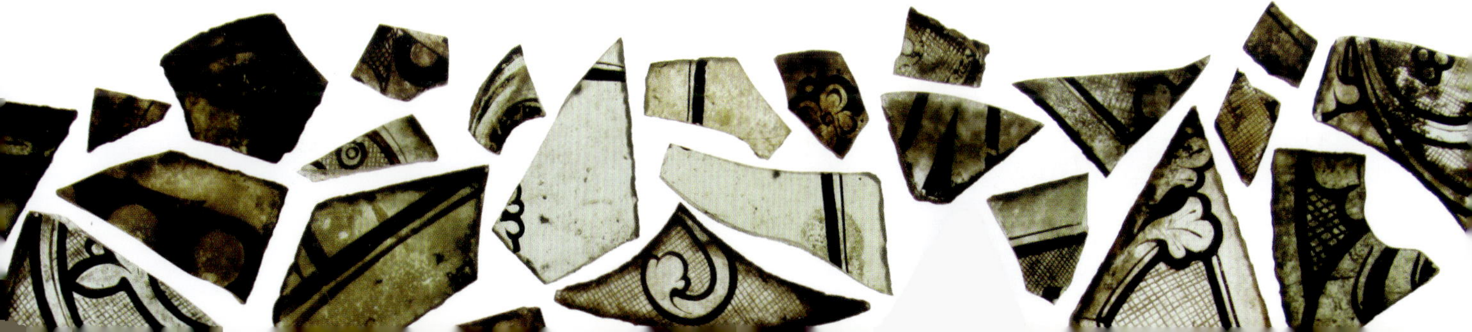

This panelling is made of imported Baltic oak, which was felled at some point between 1348 and 1364. It is believed to come from the Abbey's archive or Muniment Room, the open gallery in the south transept, where panelling with similar decoration survives *in situ*. The Muniment Room's partition wall faces the quire and is decorated with a magnificent painting of the white hart, personal badge of Richard II (1377–99).

The panelling on display retains remnants of its original decoration. It was painted red, with seven-pointed pale cream-yellow stars or suns, which were probably applied using a stencil. It consists of a door post and just over ten boards, and was probably decorated by the king's painter Gilbert Prince (d. 1396) or his successor Thomas Litlyngton (also known as Prince). Richard II's personal symbols, the white hart and radiant suns, can also be seen elsewhere in the Abbey, including on his tomb in St Edward the Confessor's Chapel (completed in 1397).

The original function of the Muniment Room and the dominant presence of the painted white hart are not easy to explain, although it has been argued that this space was used as a royal pew. Recent research has suggested that instead of the radiant sun of Richard II, the painted 'sun-in-splendour' decoration is a star motif, representing the *étoiles* (stars) on the shield of William de Colchester, Abbot of Westminster from 1386 to 1420. The abbot's symbol therefore sits below the white hart of Richard II, expressing the abbot's support for the King.

The small six-pointed gilded metal sun or star is of similar date. It was discovered under the floor of the triforium gallery when the vaults were cleaned in 2015.

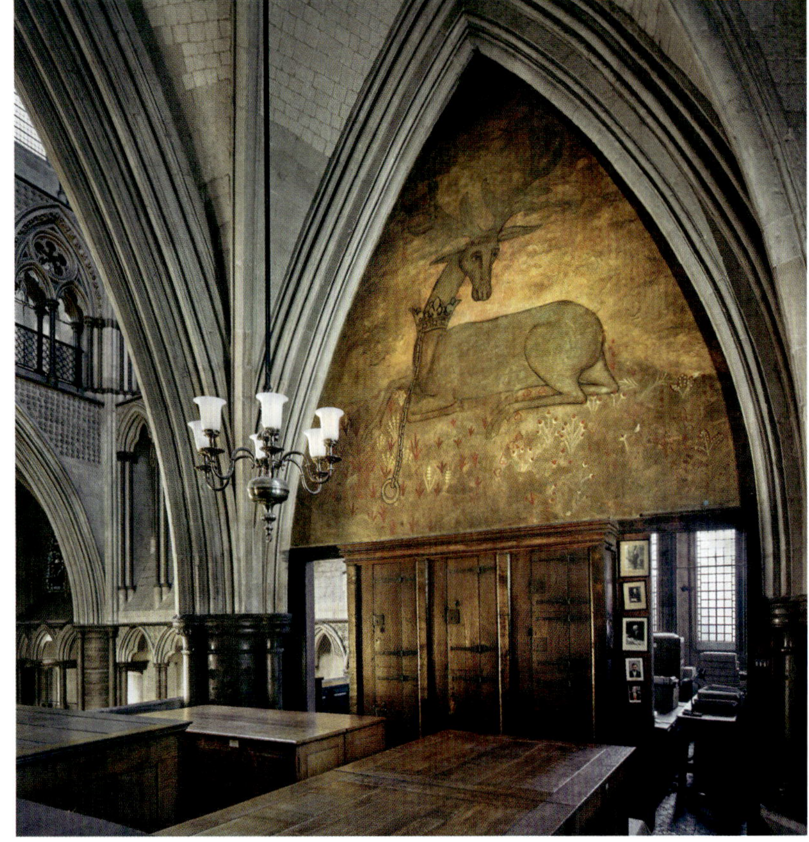

The Muniment Room looking south

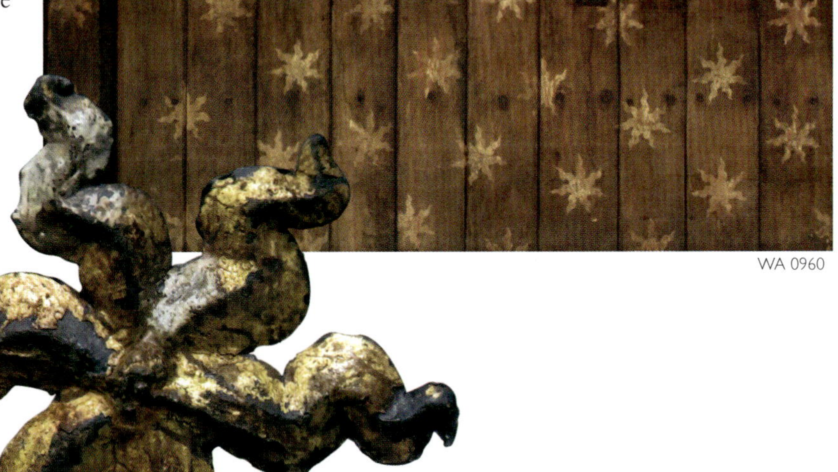

WA 0960

WA 2800

6 Buttress Beasts, about 1810

In 1503 King Henry VII celebrated his devotion to the Blessed Virgin Mary by building a new Lady Chapel on the site of Henry III's Lady Chapel. The work was overseen by either Robert Janyns or brothers Robert and William Vertue and the building was consecrated in 1516. Henry intended it as a burial place for himself, his family and his successors, and indeed he and many later monarchs are buried there.

The chapel is decorated with carved stonework both inside and out and the interior fan vaulting on the ceiling is justly celebrated. The exterior buttresses are decorated with stonework symbolic of Henry VII's reign. Their pinnacles and 'flyer arms' are crawling with seven beasts to each arm. The external statues became weather damaged and John Dart recorded in 1723 that some were removed, 'lest they should fall upon the heads of those who attend Parliament'. During the period 1809–22, further extensive external repair work was undertaken on the chapel. This began under the surveyorship of

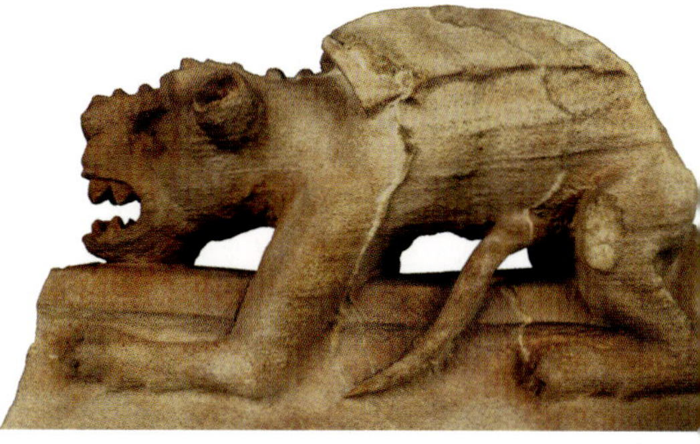

WA 1034

James Wyatt (1746–1813) and was recorded in 1808 by *The Gentleman's Magazine:* 'All the decayed and dilapidated parts are to be renewed with stone'. Many of the grotesque stone beasts on the buttress flyers (like the lion below and the dragon above) were re-carved during this campaign of restoration under the Abbey's trusted master mason, Thomas Gayfere, who had succeeded his father in the post. The carvings were made by craftsmen working in sheds on the north side of the chapel, who were highly paid for their skill. Gayfere had recommended using Bath stone for the repairs, but by the 1990s its condition had deteriorated so much that further restoration was required under the Surveyor of the Fabric, Donald Buttress.

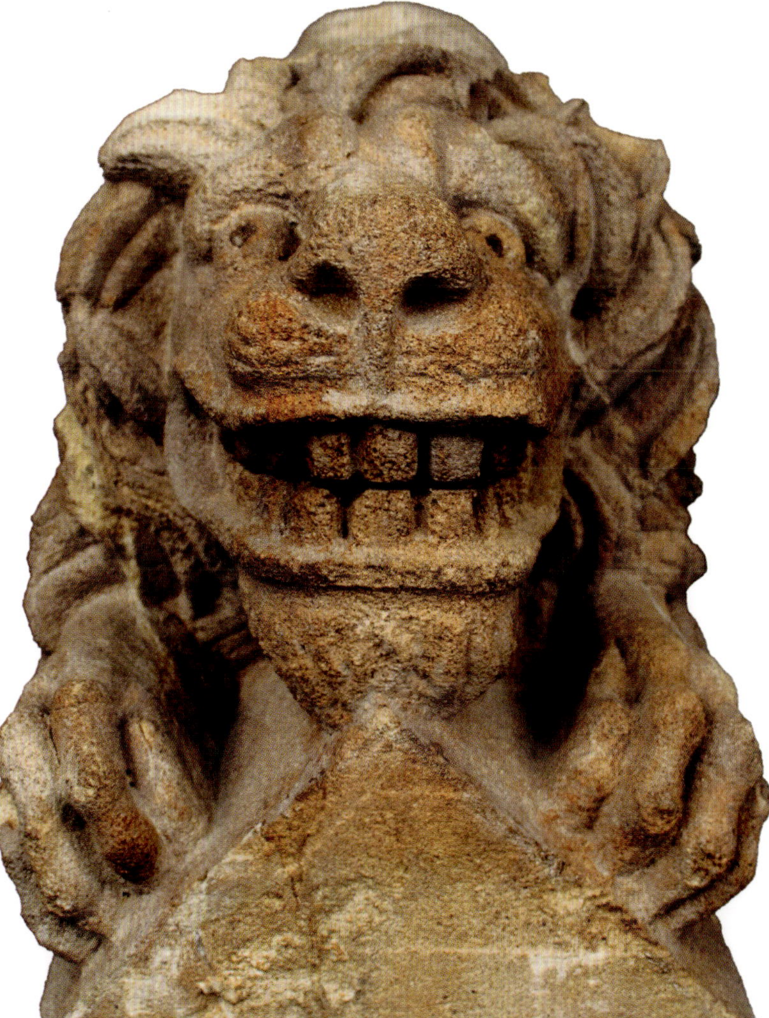

WA 1033

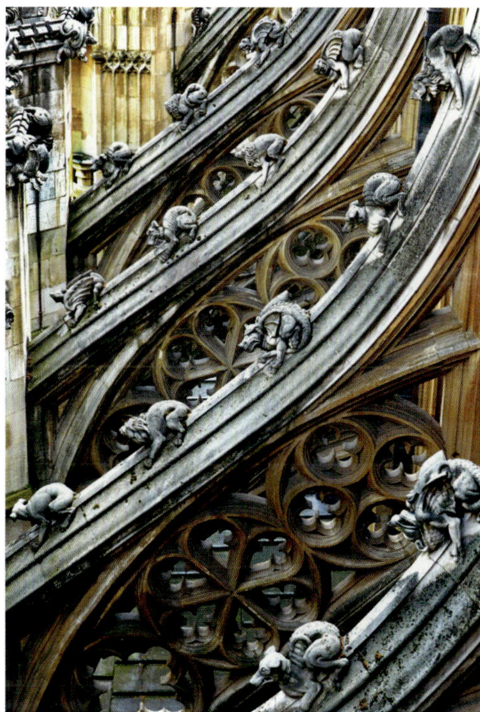

Carved beasts on the exterior of the Lady Chapel

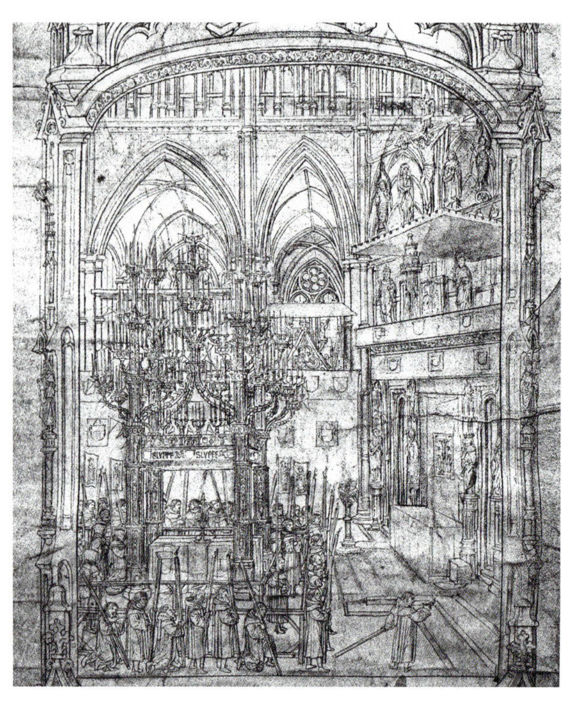

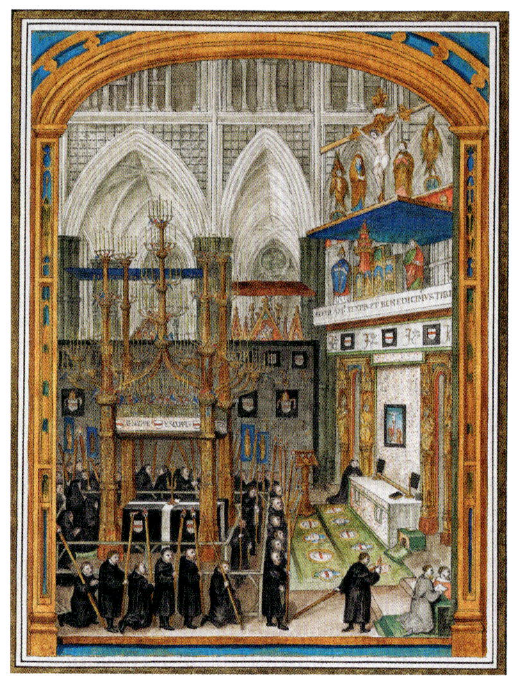

Scenes from the Roll photographed in ultraviolet light: the abbot's coffin and catafalque at his funeral (far left), and the abbot on his deathbed (below)

Left: Islip's funeral in a coloured drawing made from the Islip Roll by George Vertue, 1744 (Oxford, Bodleian Library, Gough Maps 226)

Below left: Carved head, possibly Abbot Islip, about 1500–25

7 Mortuary Roll of Abbot Islip, 1532

20

The Islip roll, which measures over 160 cm long, consists of five fine drawings on vellum, possibly a presentation copy of the mortuary (or obituary) roll of John Islip (1464–1532), Abbot of Westminster from 1500. Rolls such as these were made to record and publicise important deaths in the religious community. Usually drawn up by a monastic officer named the precentor, they were circulated to the heads of other religious houses to invite prayers for the soul of the deceased. The drawings were made in pen and ink and show scenes relating to Abbot Islip. They include two depicting the medieval Abbey, which are the only views of its interior before the monastery was closed by Henry VIII in 1540. In one of these, Islip's coffin can be seen in its temporary funerary catafalque near the High Altar, while another shows the chantry chapel which he built for his burial.

Islip was originally a monk at Westminster Abbey. In 1487 he was appointed chaplain to John Estney, Abbot of Westminster 1474–98, before becoming the last elected abbot in 1500. He oversaw building works that included the construction of Henry VII's Lady Chapel, the completion of the nave and a remodelling of the abbot's house. In 1509 he assisted at the coronation of King Henry VIII, as depicted in another of the drawings on the Islip roll.

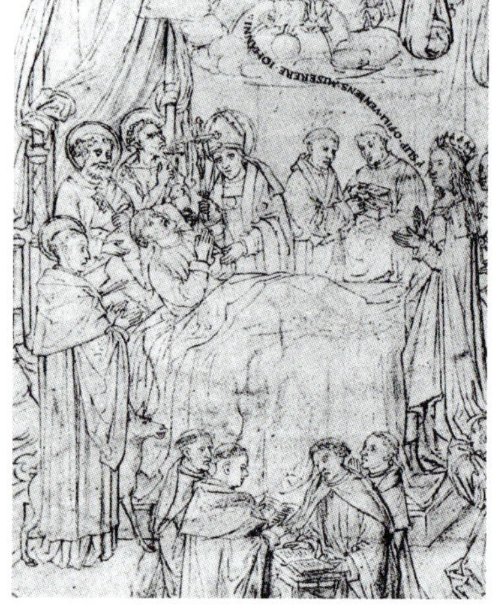

This roll is the finest example of its kind to survive in England and may have been drawn by the Flemish painter Gerard Horenbout, (d. 1540/1). Horenbout worked in various media, including stained glass and portraiture, but he specialised in manuscript illumination. He was no stranger to royal patronage, being employed by the cultured Margaret of Austria, governor of the Habsburg Netherlands, before moving to England, by at latest 1528, to work for Henry VIII.

8 Scale Model of the crossing of Westminster Abbey with a tower and spire, 1714–16

Sir Christopher Wren was appointed Westminster Abbey's Surveyor of the Fabric in 1698, with responsibility for its repair and maintenance. He oversaw re-roofing work; new glass in the transepts; a new choir screen (for which he designed the wooden obelisks on display); the installation of the impressive Whitehall Altarpiece at the Abbey's High Altar (which he had originally designed for King James II's private chapel at Whitehall Palace in 1685, parts of which are on display); and the development of a scheme to add a tower and spire to the Abbey's crossing.

The 2.4-metre-high oak and pearwood architectural model of the Abbey with a tower and spire has a scale of 1:48 (1 inch to 4 ft). Commissioned by Wren in 1714–16 to help develop his designs, it was made by the Abbey's carpentry workshop, run by widow Elizabeth Gregory. Drawings show two versions of a Gothic spire, eight-sided and twelve-sided, but the model has a twelve-sided spire, suggesting that this was Wren's preference. Wren thought that Westminster Abbey was originally intended to be finished with a tower or steeple. In a report for Dean Atterbury in 1713, he wrote: 'In my Opinion the Tower should be continued to at least as much in Height above the Roof, as it is in Breadth; and if a Spire be added to it, it will give a proper Grace to the whole Fabric, and the West-end of the City, which seems to want it.' Although work on the base of the tower started in 1725, it was only carried to the top of the roof, partly because of a shortage of funds. The spire would have measured 111 metres (365 ft) above the ground, making it the tallest in London at the time, very close in height to the dome of Wren's own St Paul's Cathedral.

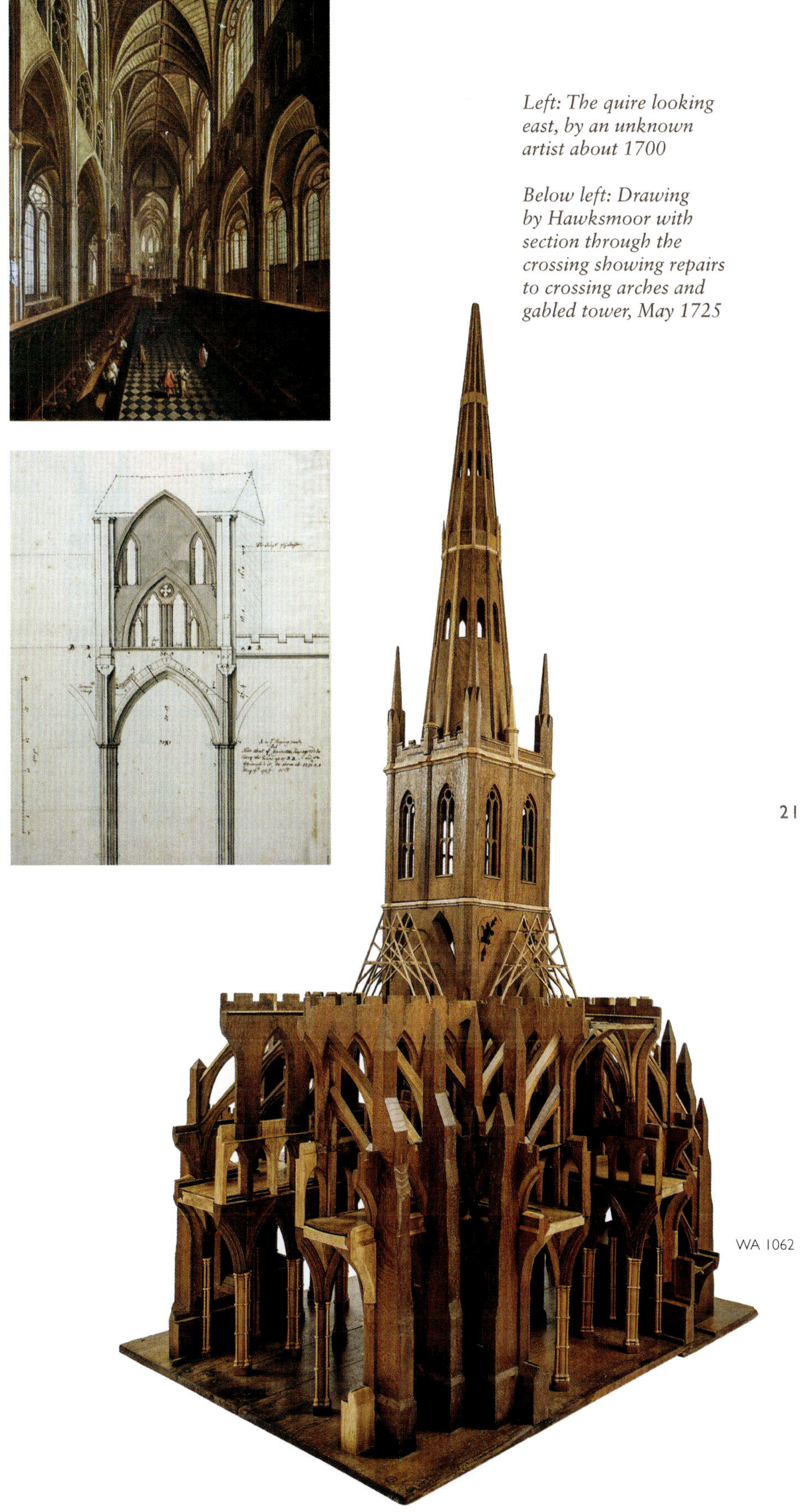

Left: The quire looking east, by an unknown artist about 1700

Below left: Drawing by Hawksmoor with section through the crossing showing repairs to crossing arches and gabled tower, May 1725

21

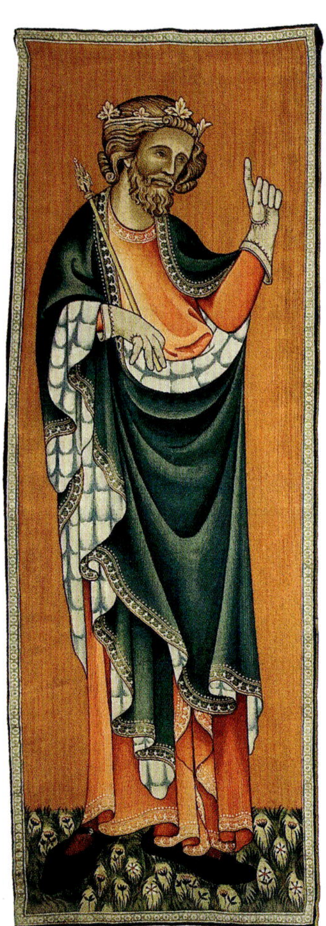
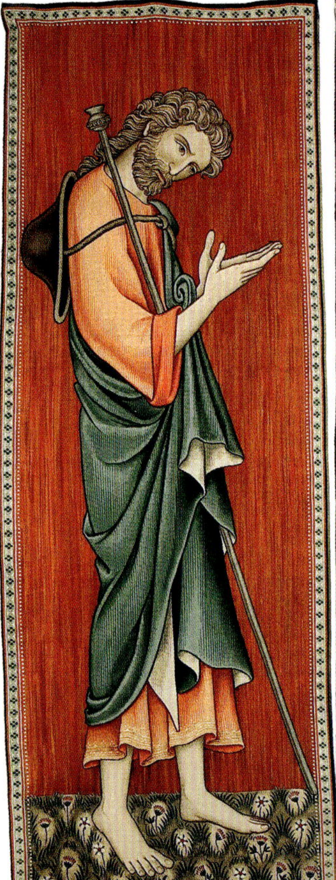
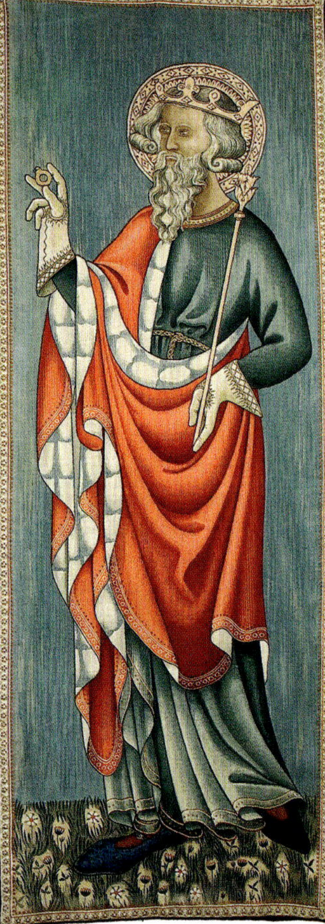

Below: The fourteenth-century sedilia on the south side of the sacrarium (sanctuary)

Opposite: Plaster model of Dr Martin Luther King Junior (1929–68)

9 Tapestry Panels: King Henry III; St John the Evangelist; St Edward the Confessor, 1910–14

These colourful tapestries were commissioned for Westminster Abbey by benefactors Henry Yates Thompson and Mr and Mrs Murray Smith in the years 1910–14. They were woven in wool and silk on a cotton warp at the Merton Abbey Tapestry Workshop, which was founded in 1881 by celebrated designer and conservationist William Morris and run by weaver-director John Henry Dearle.

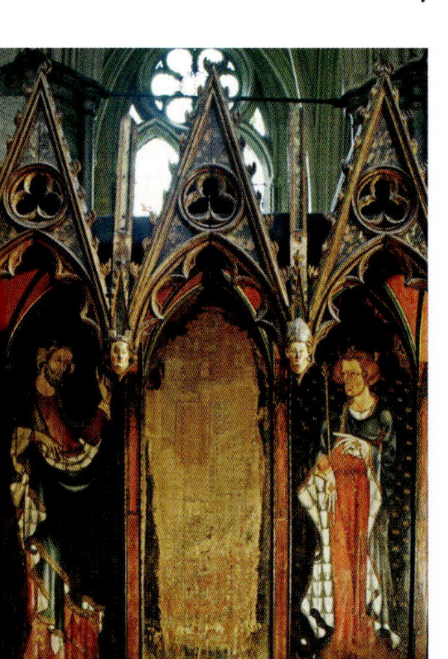

The subjects were taken from the wooden sedilia (seats for priests) next to the Abbey's High Altar, which were originally painted in about 1307, possibly by Thomas of Westminster. Running from left to right, the tapestries show Henry III (who appears on the easternmost seat of the sedilia), woven in 1911; St John the Evangelist disguised as a pilgrim, woven in 1914; and St Edward the Confessor holding out a ring, woven in 1910 (both on the south side of the sedilia, but in the painting only the king survives). The story of St Edward the Confessor and the ring is an important one for the Abbey. Legend has it that St Edward gave his ring to a beggar requesting alms, who was subsequently discovered to be St John the Evangelist. This scene is described in various accounts of the life of St Edward the Confessor and was a favourite of King Henry III. Designs for the tapestries were made by medieval historian and painter Professor E.W. Tristram whose surviving quarter life-size watercolours based on the sedilia were made in 1909.

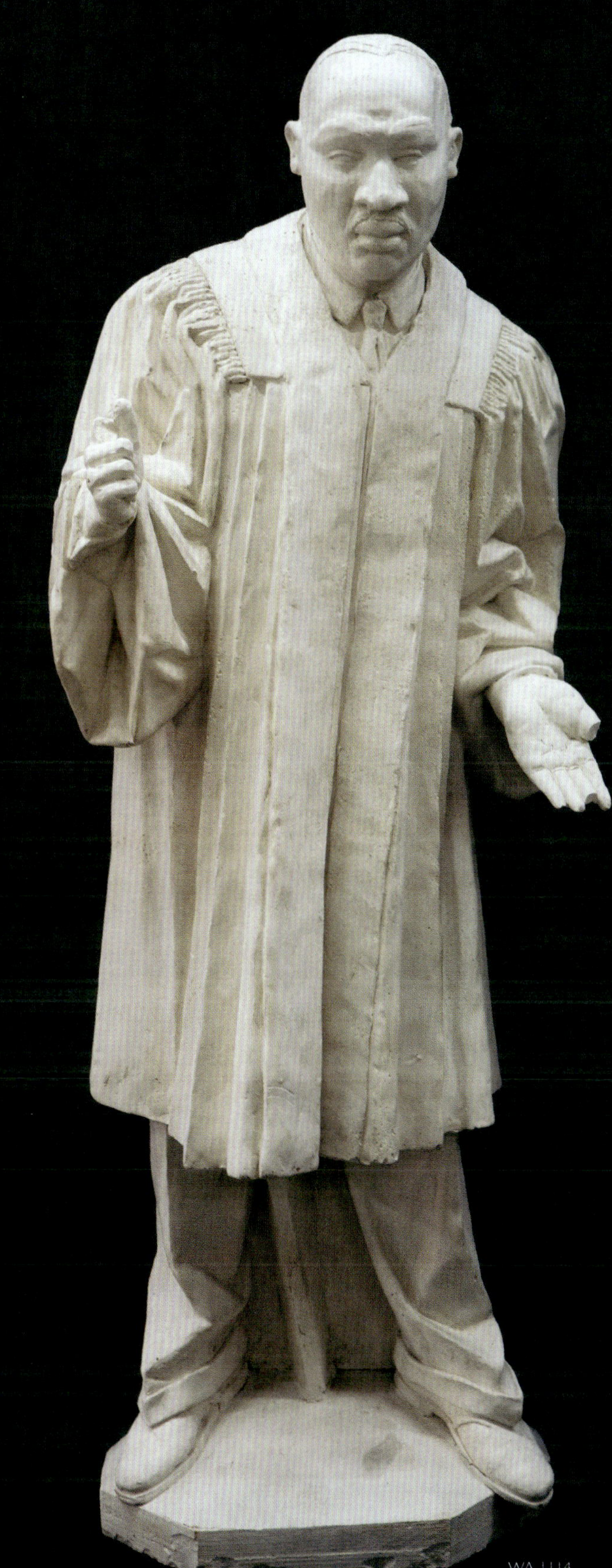

10 Modern Christian Martyrs from the Abbey's West Front, 1998

In July 1998, ten life-size stone figures of modern Christian martyrs were installed in empty niches above the Abbey's Great West Door and unveiled by Her Majesty Queen Elizabeth II. These niches were part of the west porch façade, completed by about 1450, and were originally filled with now-lost statues, for which there are no records. The new figures, chosen by the dean and chapter of Westminster after wide consultation, include martyrs from all five continents. Small figures were first modelled in clay by sculptor Tim Crawley at a scale of 1:5. Each martyr was then modelled at half life-size, based on photographs and images. Next, half life-size plaster casts (maquettes) were made of each figure, examples of which are on display.

The first of the finished full-size carved stone statues, positioned from left to right above the Great West Door, is the figure of Polish Catholic priest St Maximilian Kolbe, killed by the Nazis in the German concentration camp Auschwitz-Birkenau in 1941. Next stands Manche Masemola, killed by her parents in 1928 in the former province of Transvaal, South Africa, for her adherence to Christianity. Beside her is former Archbishop of Uganda Janani Luwum, murdered in 1977 for protesting against Idi Amin's government. Next is Queen Victoria's granddaughter, Grand Duchess Elizabeth of Russia (a saint of the Russian Orthodox church), who became a Russian Orthodox nun and was thrown down a mineshaft in 1918 during the Russian Bolshevik Revolution. She stands next to Baptist preacher and Civil Rights campaigner Dr Martin Luther King Junior, assassinated in Memphis, Tennessee in 1968. The figure next to him is St Oscar Romero, Archbishop of San Salvador, who was killed while celebrating Mass in 1980 because of his outspoken opposition to the regime. Beside him is Dietrich Bonhoeffer, the German Lutheran theologian killed by the Nazis in 1945. Next is Esther John, a Presbyterian evangelist who was mysteriously killed in her native Pakistan in 1960. Beside her is Lucian Tapiedi, an Anglican missionary killed in Papua New Guinea in 1942; and finally, Chinese pastor and evangelist Wang Zhiming, killed in the country's Cultural Revolution in 1973.

The project sought to encourage the revival of traditional craftsmanship. Donald Buttress, then Surveyor of the Fabric, commented: 'What a vindication of the mason-craftsman approach it has been and I hope it will further assist in a return in due course to the right and time-honoured principles of real restoration!'

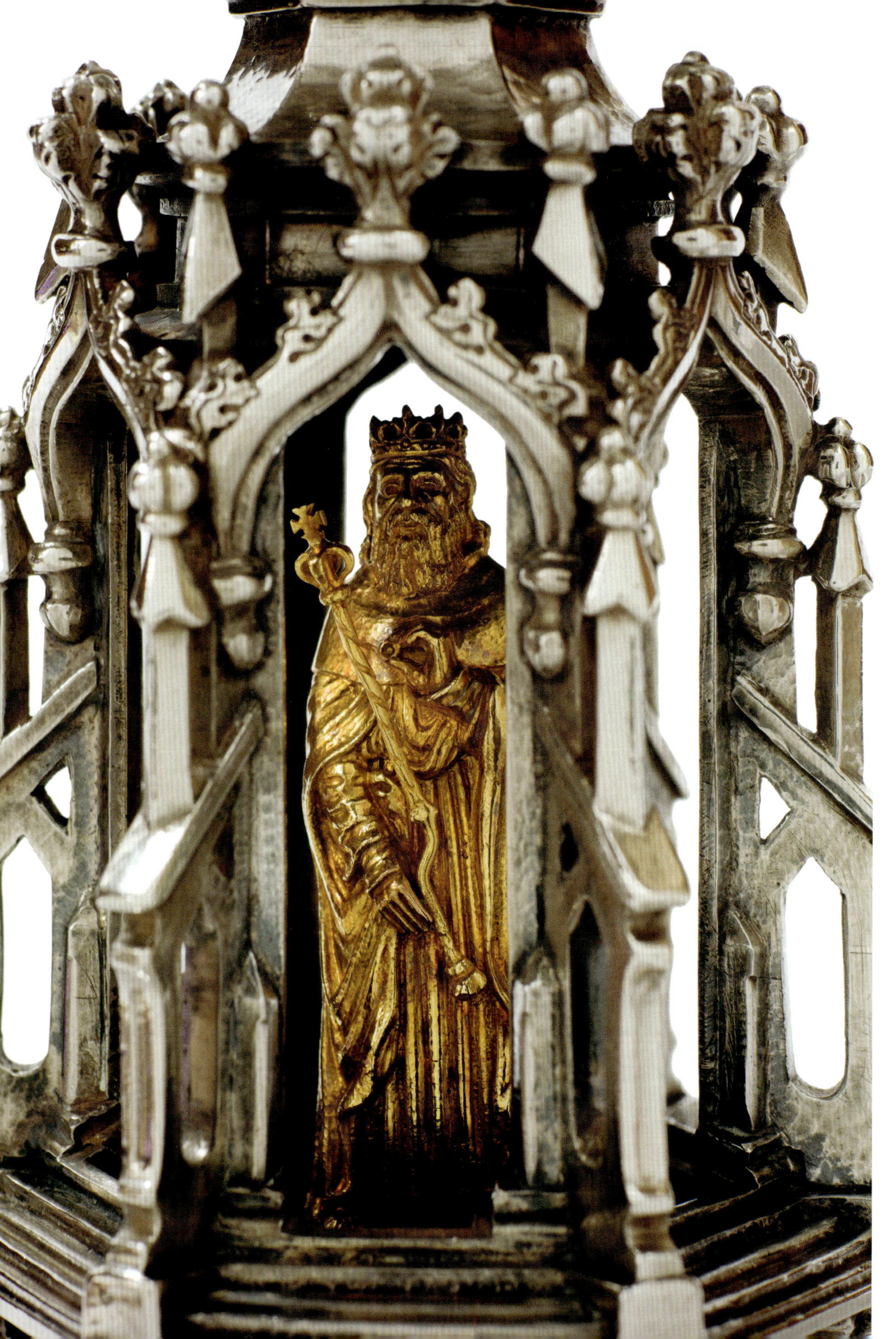

THE DAILY LIFE OF MEDIEVAL Westminster Abbey was shaped by the Rule of St Benedict, which regulated in detail the running of monasteries and the activities of their monks. Daily worship of God was at the heart of monastic life, and services at Westminster followed broadly the same pattern as those held in many hundreds of Benedictine monasteries across western Europe. Central to monastic spirituality were the 'offices', services held at fixed points throughout the day and night which gave structure and context to all other activity. The day began with the service of Matins, held around midnight, and ended with the service of Compline at around 8.00pm. The offices are often referred to as the *opus dei*, or 'work of God', and consisted principally of the recitation of the Psalms supplemented by hymns, prayers and other passages of scripture. The monks assembled in the quire for these services, which were entirely in Latin and chanted rather than spoken. During the middle ages, the monastic chants became increasingly complex and were supplemented by polyphony (music sung in more than one part). Eventually the monks employed professional musicians for some of the services, a distant forerunner of the Choir of Westminster Abbey which sings the services today.

Complementing the offices were daily celebrations of the Mass or Eucharist in ritual commemoration of the Last Supper, the meal that Jesus ate with his disciples the evening before his crucifixion. The whole community attended a daily Mass celebrated at the High Altar, but those monks who were priests also said their own Mass at one of the chapel altars. Additional Masses were said as a form of prayer for the souls of those who had died. Many of the Abbey's chapels and altars had been built or endowed for this purpose, such as the chantry chapel of Henry V and the altar associated with the tomb of Henry VII. The performance of these duties required large quantities of service books, vestments, communion plate and other liturgical ornaments, few of which survived the dissolution of the monastery in 1540.

By the fourteenth century Westminster was the richest of all the English monasteries, largely on account of its early royal patronage and its position close to the seat of government. Two indicators of its distinction were the right of the abbot to wear a mitre, and the grant of 1222 which exempted the Abbey from the jurisdiction of the Bishop of London and the Archbishop of Canterbury, placing it directly under the pope's authority.

The monastery was governed by the abbot, who was held in great respect by the monks. He was often away from the Abbey on royal or church business, and appointed a prior from among the monks to act as his deputy and oversee the domestic administration of the monastery. The Benedictine order was not 'enclosed', so with permission the monks could leave the monastery, to conduct business or visit the Abbey's estates. Monks who were intellectually gifted were sent to university at Oxford.

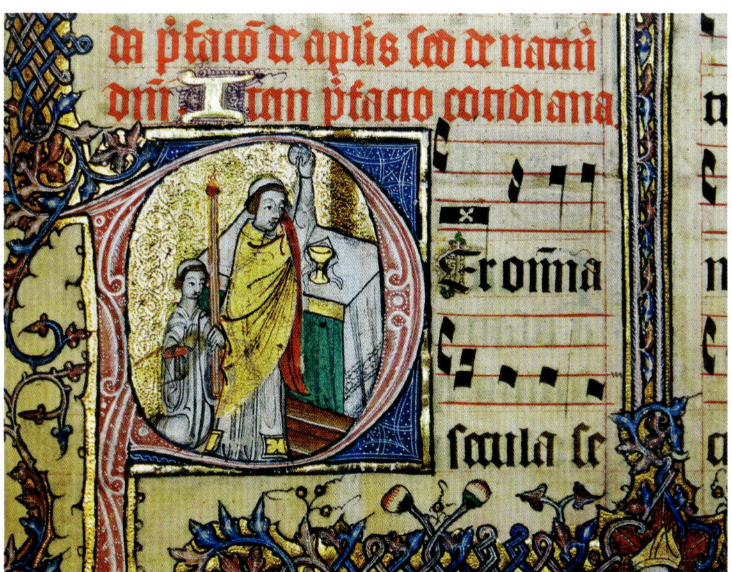

Within the monastery a sophisticated system of administration developed, with individual monks called obedientiaries having oversight of key aspects of daily life. The infirmarer cared for the sick, the cellarer supplied food and drink, and the sacrist provided the requisites of worship (vestments, plate, candles). Extensive records kept by these and other officials survive among the Abbey's muniments (archives) and give valuable detail about monastic life at Westminster.

All monasteries required certain ancillary buildings. The cloisters housed the library and were used for recreation. The chapter house and the dormitory were in the east cloister range and the refectory was off the south cloister. There was a granary, a bakery and many other additional buildings. The site was enclosed by a precinct wall, much of which survives, and a small town grew up around the monastery, served by the parish church of St Margaret.

The monks left Westminster at the dissolution of the monastery in January 1540, and for a while the Abbey was a second cathedral in the diocese of London. Mary I revived the monastery in 1556, but her early death brought Westminster's monastic tradition to an end. When Elizabeth I established the Abbey as a collegiate church in May 1560, a new pattern of life developed. The dean and chapter who now governed the Abbey had two main duties: the daily worship of God and the education of 40 scholars. To enrich worship, there was a choir of boy choristers and singing men, and an organist. The Abbey's day was now shaped by the singing of Matins and Evensong, services which recalled and drew on the ancient pattern of the monastic offices, but in a simplified form.

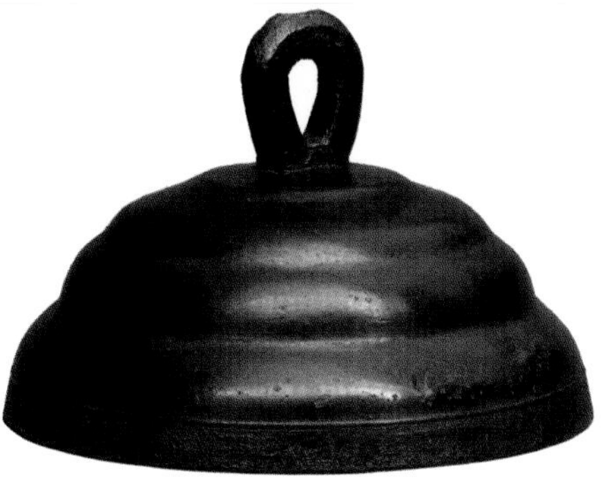

Left: Refectory or 'frater' bell, struck like a gong to call the monks to meals

Below: Monk's shoe made in leather, about 1400

Elizabeth I regarded Westminster Abbey with special favour. Under her patronage the Abbey used music and ceremonial to a degree that was rarely practised elsewhere. This Westminster tradition continued into the seventeenth century and is reflected in the dean and chapter's wearing of copes, vestments which had mostly been abandoned as 'popish' by other churches. One consequence of this conservative tradition was that in 1614 the House of Commons, objecting to the use of wafers rather than ordinary bread in the Abbey's communion service, chose to worship instead in St Margaret's church. This inaugurated the relationship between St Margaret's and Parliament which continues to this day.

Following Charles I's execution in 1649, the Abbey once more entered uncertain times. Under the Commonwealth, Presbyterianism was established and the Church of England was officially abolished. The Dean of Westminster, the prebendaries (canons) and the Abbey's musicians were ejected from their posts and the Abbey was run by a committee appointed by Parliament. Little is known about worship in the Abbey at this time, but sermons (usually of considerable length) were regularly preached in the church and published afterwards.

A new dean and chapter re-assumed governance of the Abbey soon after the Restoration of Charles II in 1660. Previous patterns of worship were also restored, and Charles II's coronation followed in 1661. The dean and chapter quickly re-established the choir and provided vestments and plate to replace those lost during the interregnum. *The Book of Common Prayer*, issued in 1662, set the worshipping pattern of the Church of England for several centuries to come. The Abbey's worship followed

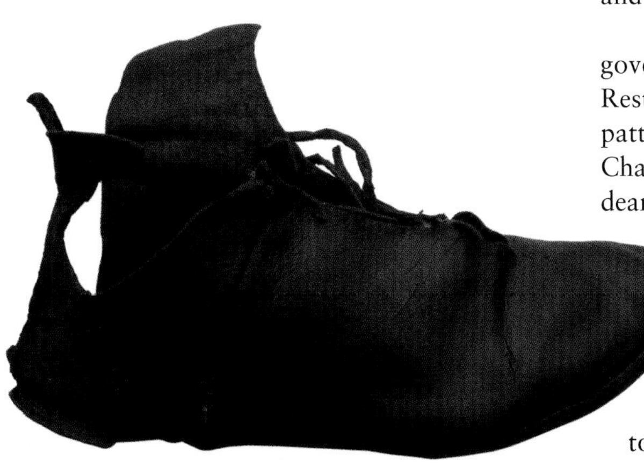

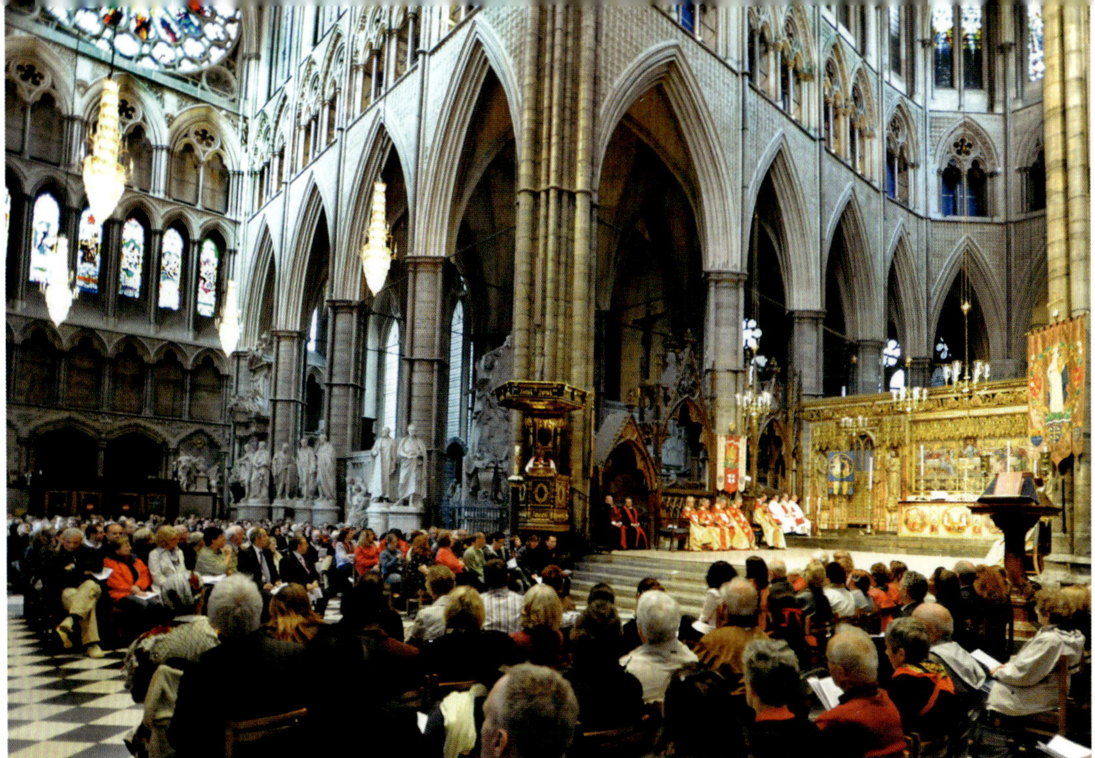

an established routine, with Matins (morning prayer) and Evensong sung by the choir and Holy Communion (Eucharist) celebrated on some Sundays and on saints' days. Members of the Church of England were required to receive Holy Communion at Easter and on two other occasions annually. The large flagons among the service plate of both the Abbey and St Margaret's were used to accommodate the quantity of communion wine required at Easter and other festivals as a result.

Throughout the late seventeenth and eighteenth centuries national 'fast days' commemorated anniversaries such as the accession of the monarch and the Gunpowder Plot. On these occasions the House of Lords came to the Abbey to hear a sermon, while the Commons (maintaining the custom begun in 1614) went to St Margaret's, a tradition which only died out in the early years of the nineteenth century. It is difficult to know what the Abbey's ordinary services were like by this time or how many people attended them. The dean and chapter certainly maintained the choral tradition, although probably only a handful of worshippers attended on a weekday. In January 1858, however, Sunday evening services were introduced in the nave and attracted huge crowds from the start. They continue to be held in the twenty-first century.

In the twentieth century there were many changes to the style of the Abbey's worship; some of these reflected liturgical developments in the wider church, such as making the Eucharist, rather than Matins, the principal Sunday service. Another significant innovation was the development of 'special services' to mark national events or anniversaries. Some of these are annual occasions with long histories (the Commonwealth Day Service, ANZAC Day and Battle of Britain Sunday), but many more are single occasions. Some respond to world events, such as the World Trade Center attack in 2001 or the terrorist attack in Westminster in 2017, but other services have celebrated the lives of notable national figures.

An important priority for the dean and chapter is to ensure that those visiting the Abbey as tourists understand that it is a working church. Visitors are asked to pause for a moment of prayer each hour, and the lunchtime Eucharist takes place at the nave altar while sightseeing continues around it. Visitors are welcome to join the service if they wish, and many do. The exhibits in this section of The Queen's Diamond Jubilee Galleries reflect the 1,000-year history of this place of worship. Artefacts are occasionally removed from display in order to be used, a further reminder of the Abbey's continuing spiritual life.

27

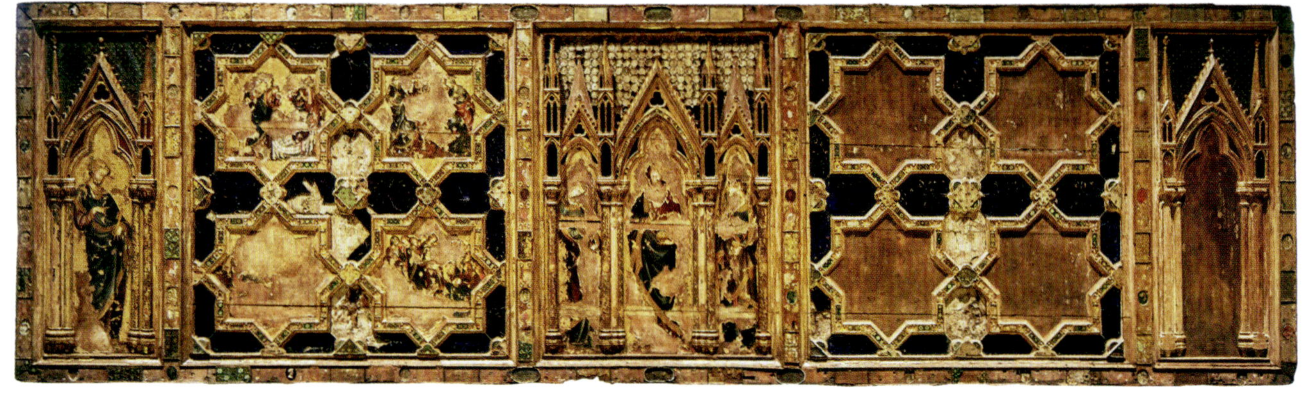

WA 0881

1 The Westminster Retable, 1259–69

The retable was almost certainly the high altarpiece of Henry III's Abbey and is England's oldest surviving altarpiece, though at first sight it can be difficult to visualise what it must originally have looked like. Made of painted and gilded wood, but with decorative metalwork, enamel, glass and other materials adding to its artistic complexity, it would have been an opulent and beautiful work of art. In the central panel, beneath Gothic arches, stands a figure of Jesus Christ, flanked by the Virgin Mary and St John the Evangelist and with his right hand raised in blessing. His left hand holds an orb representing the world, which is painted with remarkable miniatures of the sun and moon, water and a boat, animals and birds. On the extreme left is a figure of St Peter, the Abbey's patron saint, holding the key to heaven in his left hand. The lost painting in the equivalent position on the right-hand side is believed to have shown St Paul.

Two intermediate panels each contain four medallions. Those on the right have lost their paintings, but some of the exquisite thirteenth-century paintings of the miracles of Jesus survive in the left-hand medallions. From top left, clockwise, they show Christ raising to life the daughter of Jairus (a Jewish elder); the healing of the man born blind; and the feeding of the five thousand. Only some traces of the fourth painting survive.

Although the retable was not destroyed at the Reformation, it was badly treated in the following centuries; it became part of a display case for funeral effigies and was partly painted over when William Pitt's effigy was placed in the display case in 1778. Fortunately it was rescued in 1827 and framed, but it was not until 1998 that a lengthy programme of conservation work began and revealed the true splendour of this remarkable medieval treasure.

Details from the Westminster Retable: two figures from the feeding of the five thousand (left) and the orb held in Christ's left hand

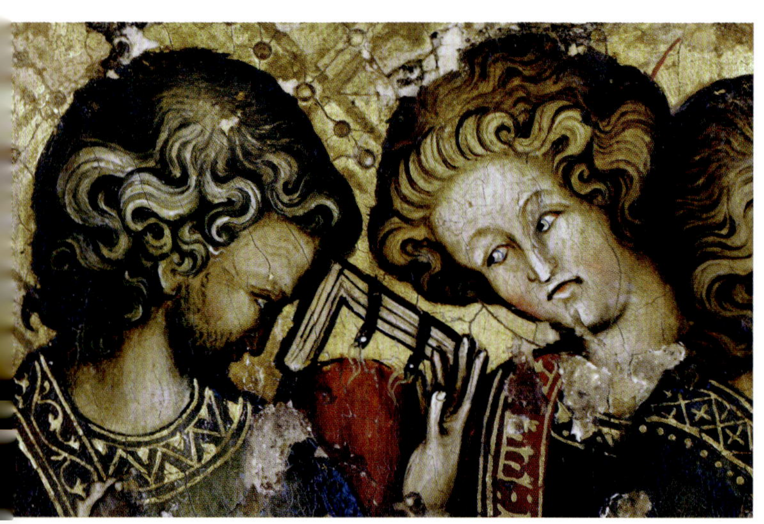

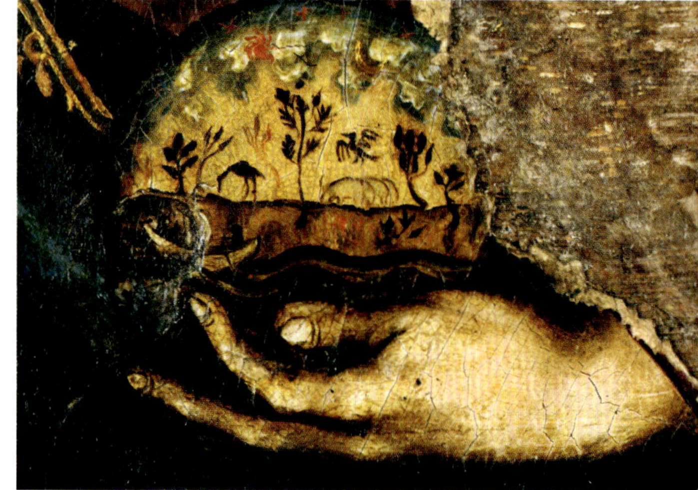

2 The Litlyngton Missal, 1383–84

This magnificent Latin manuscript, one of the largest surviving English medieval manuscripts, is richly decorated with coloured inks and gold leaf. In two volumes since it was rebound in 1806, the 682 pages of the missal contain the readings and prayers used at the celebration of the Mass, along with a calendar of festivals and saints' days. It also includes services particularly associated with the Abbey, such as the coronation order and observances for the feasts of St Edward the Confessor. Nicholas Litlyngton, Abbot of Westminster 1362–86, commissioned the manuscript for use at the High Altar of the Abbey and paid for it from his personal funds as abbot. His coat of arms and initials appear at various points in the manuscript to remind the user of his involvement.

From the Abbey's records we know that the manuscript was made between 1383 and 1384 and that four individuals worked on it. A scribe called Thomas Preston laid out the work and wrote the text. Two unknown artists then painted the 62 illuminated initials and the numerous decorative borders. A third artist produced a magnificent crucifixion scene (right), the only full-page illumination in the missal. Thomas Preston lived in the monastery while the work was in hand and subsequently joined the Abbey as a monk, but nothing more is known of the other artists. Most of the Abbey's service books were destroyed at the dissolution of the monastery in 1540. It is not certain why this one survived, but the need for the Abbey to preserve records of the coronation liturgy may have been a factor.

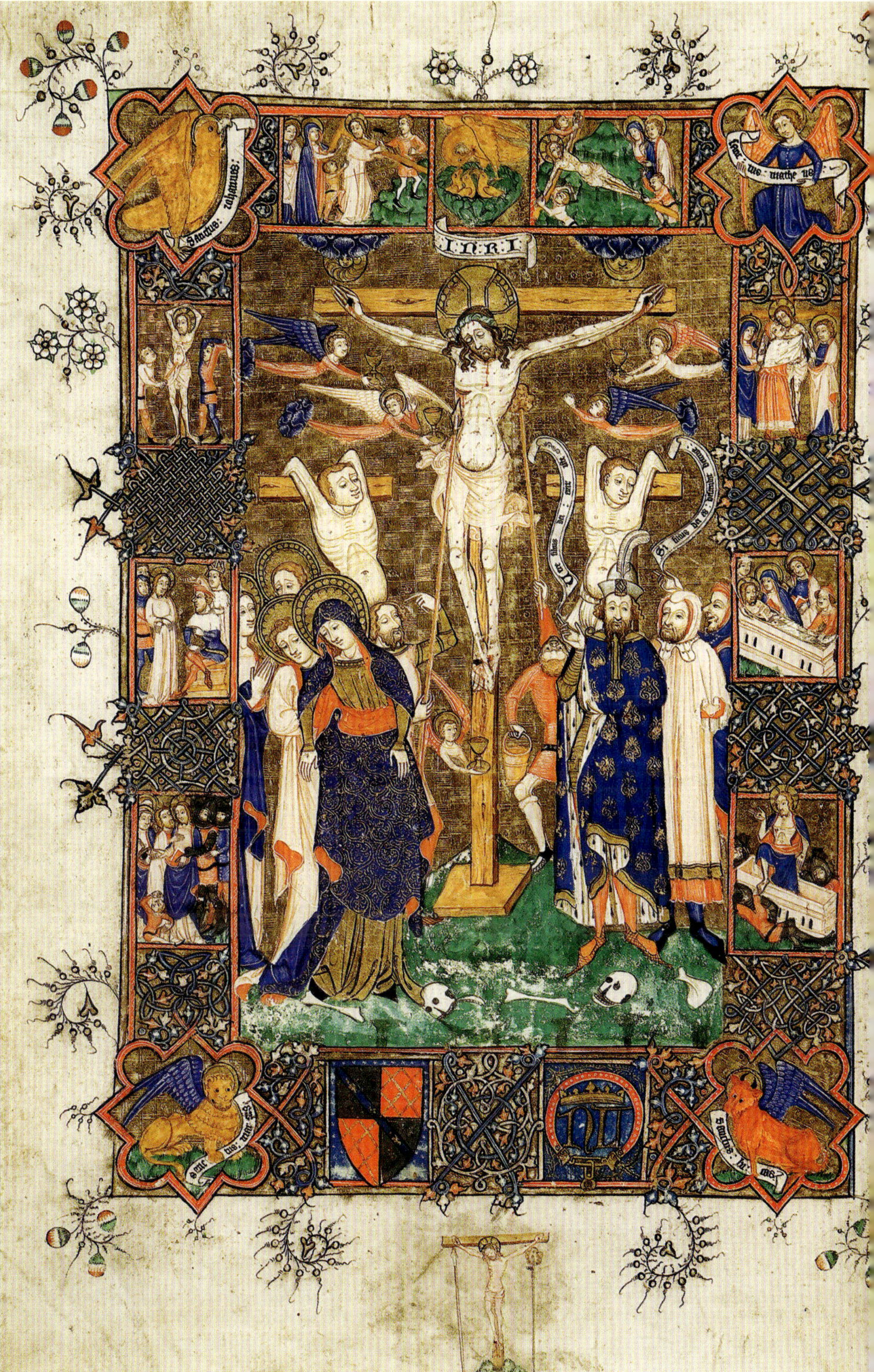

3 Treble Bell, about 1310, and Bell, 1742

At medieval Westminster Abbey, the tolling of bells regulated the pattern of worship, work and study that made up the monastic day. Different bells were rung to indicate specific events and monks were adept at distinguishing between the sounds. Much later the Anglican *Book of Common Prayer* (1662) required clergy to ring the church bell before saying morning and evening prayer. The earliest reference to bells at Westminster is an order of 1230 to Edward of Westminster, to make a bell for the Abbey bigger than any he had made before. The following year he made a smaller bell in tune with it.

In the middle ages a detached belfry stood on the north side of the Abbey, but since the 1520s bells have hung in the north-west tower, and there is now a 'ring' of ten. They can be tolled individually as a call to prayer or to mark a death, or rung in elaborate sequences, a practice known as 'change ringing'. Two bells are displayed in the Galleries. The oldest (right) dates from the early decades of the fourteenth century and was made by Richard Wymbish (active as a bell founder from 1290). It is inscribed with a Latin prayer that translates as 'Christ, hear us'. Bells often carry inscriptions or are given names. The smaller bell (top left) is inscribed 'Tho[ma]s Lester made me 1742' and used to hang externally in the gable of the south transept. Known as the 'morning bell', it was probably chimed to announce morning service.

WA 0880

WA 0879

4 Abbot's or Bishop's Crosier

Since the seventh century, bishops (and sometimes abbots) have carried a rod or staff, called a crosier, as a symbol of office, its form varying in different parts of the Christian church. In Eastern Orthodox churches, the bishop's crosier is a rod surmounted by a cross and flanked by serpents, but in the Roman Catholic Church and the Church of England the crosier ends in a shepherd's crook. It symbolises the bishop's duty to care for his people as a shepherd tends his flock, in emulation of Jesus the 'Good Shepherd'.

The medieval Abbots of Westminster had the right to carry a crosier and also to wear a mitre (the liturgical hat also more often associated with bishops). It is impossible to be sure whether this late medieval crosier belonged to a bishop or an abbot. It was uncovered in 1879 in St John the Baptist's Chapel, close to the graves of both Thomas Ruthall (d. 1523), who had been Bishop of Durham, and of Richard Harweden (d. 1440), who was Abbot of Westminster. Crosiers were often made in precious metal and richly decorated; this wooden example is in a simpler style but was probably originally painted to make it more ornate.

30

WA 0870

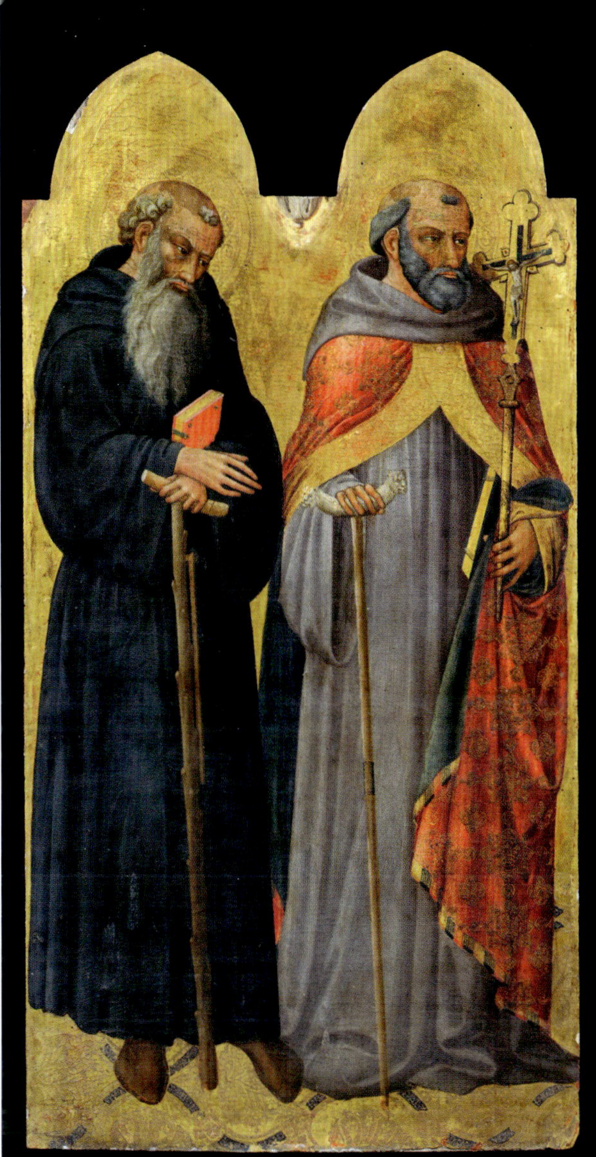

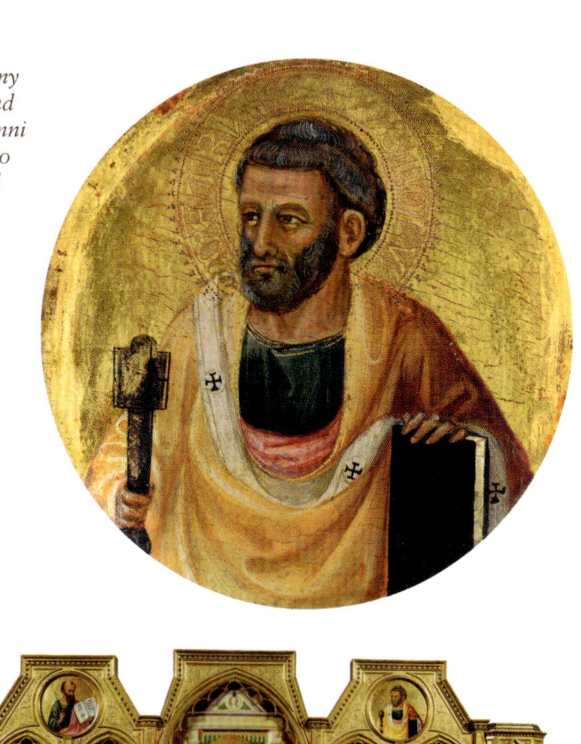

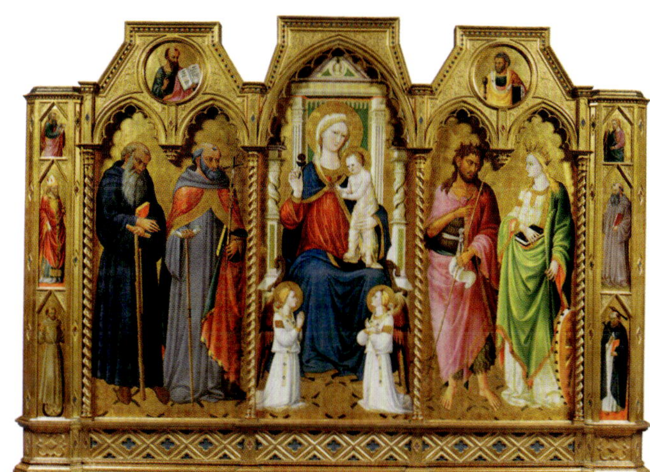

WA 0045

5 The Virgin Mary and the Christ Child flanked by Saints, about 1434

Not all the Abbey's medieval treasures are linked with its own early history. This altarpiece, by the Italian artist Bicci di Lorenzo (1375–1452), was only acquired for the Abbey in 1947. It was originally made for a chapel in the church of Santa Trinità in Florence but disappeared in the early nineteenth century, probably when a number of churches were despoiled during the Napoleonic occupation of the city.

Just as artworks in the medieval Abbey frequently depicted St Peter (the Abbey's patron) and St Edward the Confessor (the Abbey's saintly royal founder), so this painting too reflects the particular context for which it was painted. The church of Santa Trinità belonged to monks of the Vallumbrosan order and the chapel where

the altarpiece hung was dedicated to the order's founder, St Giovanni Gualberto. He appears in the left-hand panel (closest to the Virgin) alongside St Anthony Abbot, another saint particularly revered by the Vallumbrosans. The figures of St John the Baptist and St Catherine of Alexandria would also have been easily recognised by medieval worshippers as would Sts Peter (with a key) and Paul in the two roundels. Further saints are depicted in the outer pillars: Matthew, Nicholas and Francis on the left; Luke, James the Less and Peter Martyr on the right.

The altarpiece was bought from a Florentine family by Lord Crawford in 1872 and acquired at auction in 1946 by Lord Lee of Fareham (d. 1947), who bequeathed it to the Abbey.

During the Commonwealth period (from the execution of Charles I in 1649 until the Restoration in 1660), the Church of England was abolished and Presbyterian forms of worship were introduced. Many clergy were ejected from office and communion plate regarded as unnecessarily decorative was destroyed. Westminster Abbey was no exception; when the dean and chapter were restored in 1660 new plate of fine quality, marked with the shield of St Edward the Confessor, was quickly acquired. The Abbey's finest communion plate, however, arrived in 1671, when John Sudbury, one of the Abbey's prebendaries (canons) and later Dean of Durham, presented a pair of silver-gilt communion cups and patens (covers), decorated in relief known as *repoussé* work (below right).

The bowls of the cups display the arms of St Edward, set amid cherubs, acanthus leaves and other floral designs, and the patens too display the Confessor's arms. The maker, identified only by the initials 'R.A.' was probably Robert Alvey. A pair of flagons (right) and a magnificent alms dish (below) were added subsequently, decorated in the same style as the cups and made by the goldsmith John Richardson. These are dated 1684–85 and were bought by the dean and chapter with money given to them by Edward Carey following his appointment as high bailiff of Westminster. On special occasions, such as royal weddings, this seventeenth-century plate and other plate from the Abbey collection is displayed on the High Altar and the tomb of Anne of Cleves on the south side of the sanctuary.

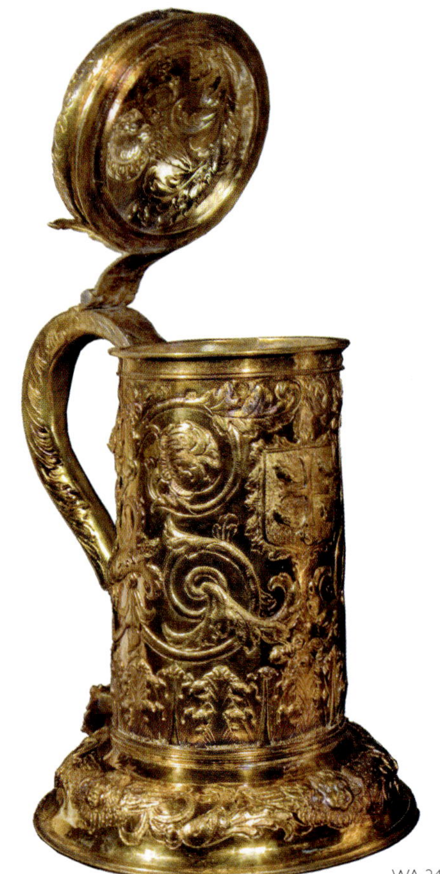

WA 2438

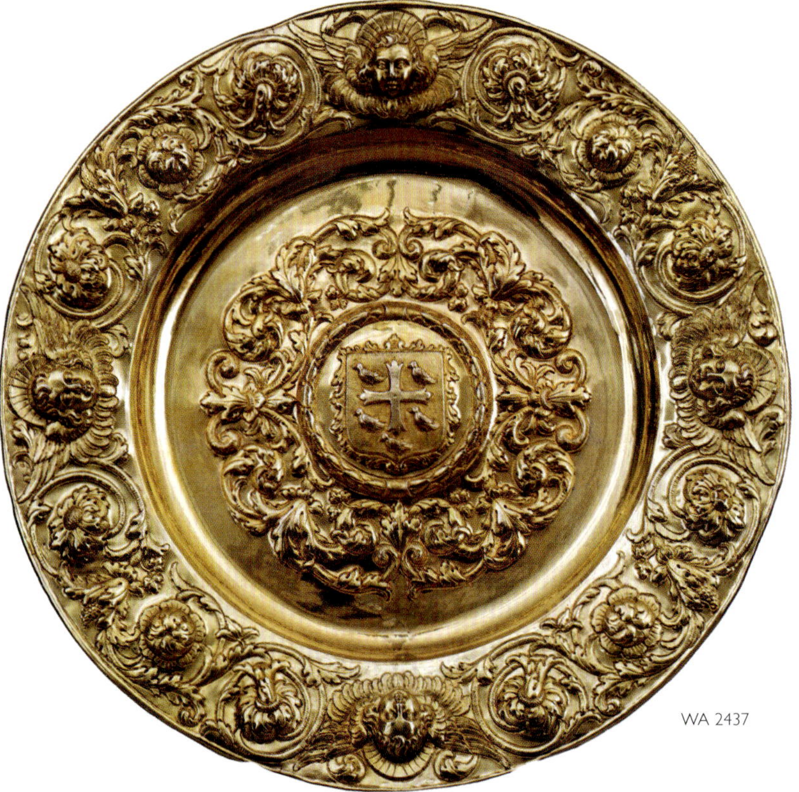

WA 2437

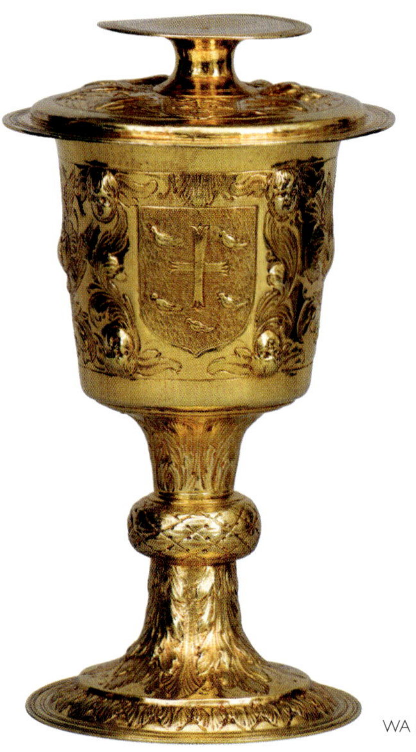

WA 2818

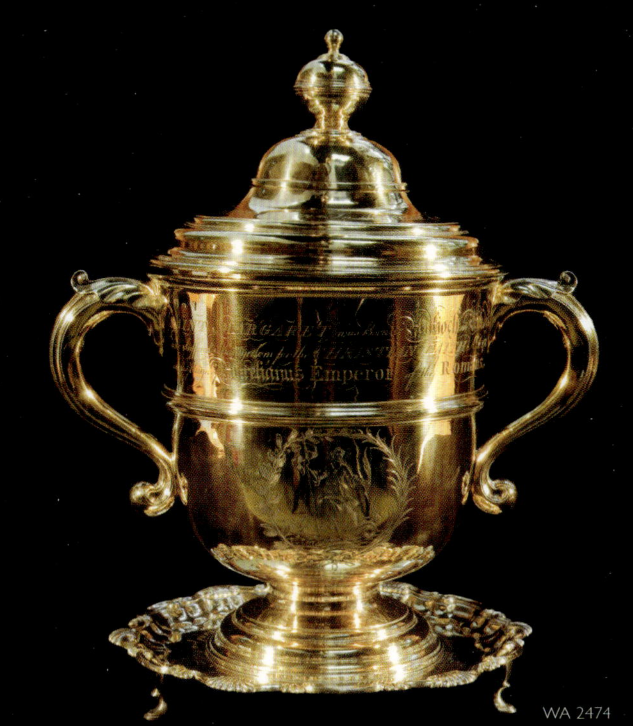

7 Cup, Cover and Salver, 1710 and 1742

This two-handled cup and lid dates from 1710 and was presented to the two churchwardens (elected officials) of St Margaret's church in 1764. At this date churchwardens often served only a year in office but Samuel Peirson, donor of the cup, had been elected seven times in succession, serving during a particularly testing time for the parish. In 1758, following the rebuilding of the decaying east wall of the church, the churchwardens purchased and installed in the east window some early-sixteenth-century stained glass (still in place today) which depicts the crucifixion of Jesus. The dean and chapter of Westminster, who claimed certain rights of jurisdiction over St Margaret's, objected that the glass displayed idolatrous images and that the parish vestry (the churchwardens and other elected officials) were required to seek the dean and chapter's licence or 'faculty' before making a change of this kind to the building. They began a legal suit against the church, which ran on for four years until eventually the dean and chapter dropped their claim. Peirson's gift of the cup, which was to be used by the vestry at 'parochial entertainments' (i.e. dinners), was perhaps partly designed to commemorate this vindication of the parish officers' actions. Three years later he presented the accompanying stand. The cup would have been used as a 'loving cup', from which each diner would drink ceremoniously in turn, as a pledge of fellowship and solidarity.

8 Beadle's Mace, 1758

Beadles were parish church officials who kept order and carried out other official duties. Sometimes, like Mr Bumble, the unpleasant beadle in Charles Dickens's *Oliver Twist*, they oversaw a parish workhouse or were associated with other charitable functions in the parish. This impressive mace is one of a set of four made for St Margaret's church in 1758. The opulent design reflects the importance of St Margaret's, which had an extensive parish and a large population that included many wealthy residents. The silver orb at the end of the wooden rod displays the coat of arms of the City of Westminster and is surmounted by a figure of St Margaret of Antioch, patron of the parish church. The inscription names the churchwardens at the time the maces were acquired. They were William Rusted and Samuel Peirson, donor of the loving cup described opposite.

Among the occasions when the beadles would have carried these maces was the annual 'beating the bounds', when parish officials walked ceremonially round the parish boundary. It was important for the boundaries to be clearly defined, as residents not only had the right to be married or buried in the parish church, but could also be required to pay local taxes or contribute to church repairs. One of the maces remains in regular use today and is used by the St Margaret's vergers to lead processions in the church and at events like the opening of the annual Field of Remembrance in St Margaret's churchyard.

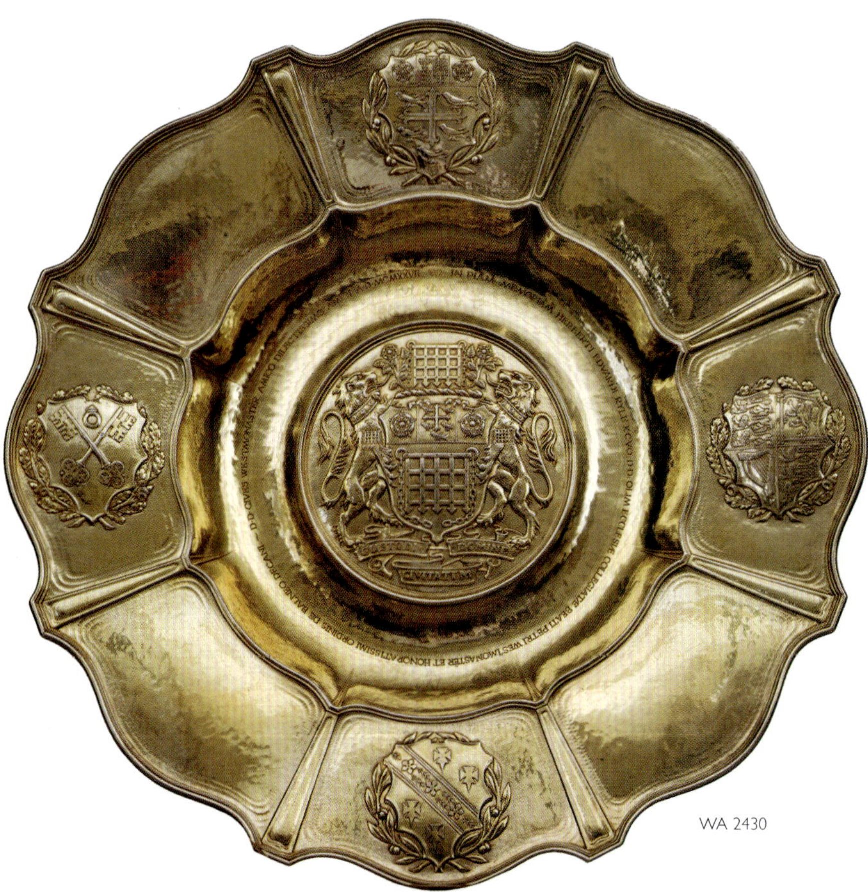

WA 2470

WA 2430

9 Two Alms Dishes, 1691–92 and 1928

Members of congregations support the church's work with gifts of money, or 'alms'. *The Book of Common Prayer* of 1662, the principal service book of the Church of England until the twentieth century, directed that alms should be collected in a 'decent bason'. This might be a simple brass plate or an elaborate dish of precious metal, depending on the wealth of the church concerned. The Last Supper was a popular subject for decoration on an alms dish because it reminded worshippers of the self-sacrifice of Christ. An early example, dating from 1664, is among the communion plate associated with the Crown Jewels.

The Last Supper alms dish displayed in The Queen's Diamond Jubilee Galleries (top left) is later in date (1691–92); it was made by a noted London goldsmith, Francis Garthorne, whose other work included commissions for William III and Mary II. Also displayed in the Galleries is one of four matching dishes presented to the Abbey by the City of Westminster in 1928. These are another example of the work of Omar Ramsden, whose Edward the Confessor chalice is described opposite. The dishes are a distinctive shape and have the arms of the City of Westminster in the centre. Around the rim are the arms of Westminster Abbey, the royal arms, the arms of Herbert Ryle, Dean of Westminster 1911–25, and a shield displaying the cross keys of St Peter and the ring of St Edward the Confessor. A Latin inscription records that the plates commemorate Dean Ryle.

10 Chalice and Paten with a figure of St Edward the Confessor, 1925

This beautiful chalice (communion cup) and paten are by the English silversmith Omar Ramsden (1873–1939). He produced designs for many churches in the early twentieth century, often influenced by late medieval and Renaissance metalwork. The plain bowl of this cup has a base of wavy lines to represent running water, with four superimposed panels showing the symbols of the four Evangelists. Underneath is a delicate canopy, supported by buttresses reminiscent of those supporting the Abbey and containing a gold figure of St Edward the Confessor.

On the base of the chalice are shields of gold, with heraldry worked in enamelled colours. The large shields are the royal arms, the arms of Westminster Abbey and the arms of Herbert Ryle, Dean of Westminster 1911–25. Twelve smaller shields are the arms of kings and queens buried in the Abbey, with the arms of St Edward the Confessor and the cross keys of St Peter. A Latin inscription on the base can be translated as 'I alone create all things from the beginning'. The paten has a central figure of Christ and further shields of St Peter and St Edward. These pieces were presented to the Abbey for use in St Edward the Confessor's Chapel in 1925. They were the gift of the Girls' Friendly Society, a philanthropic organisation for girls and young women which celebrated its fiftieth anniversary that year.

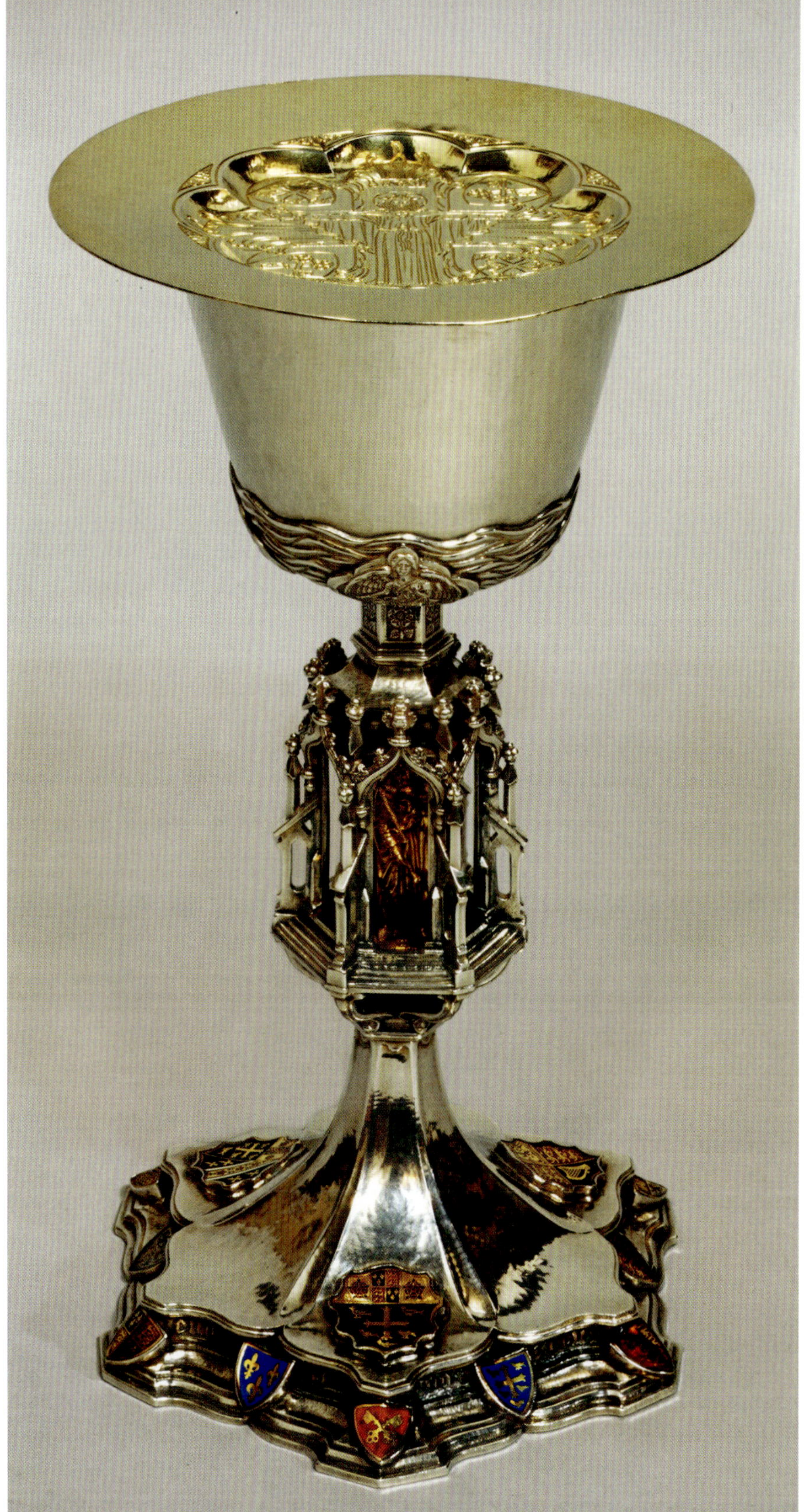

WA 2773

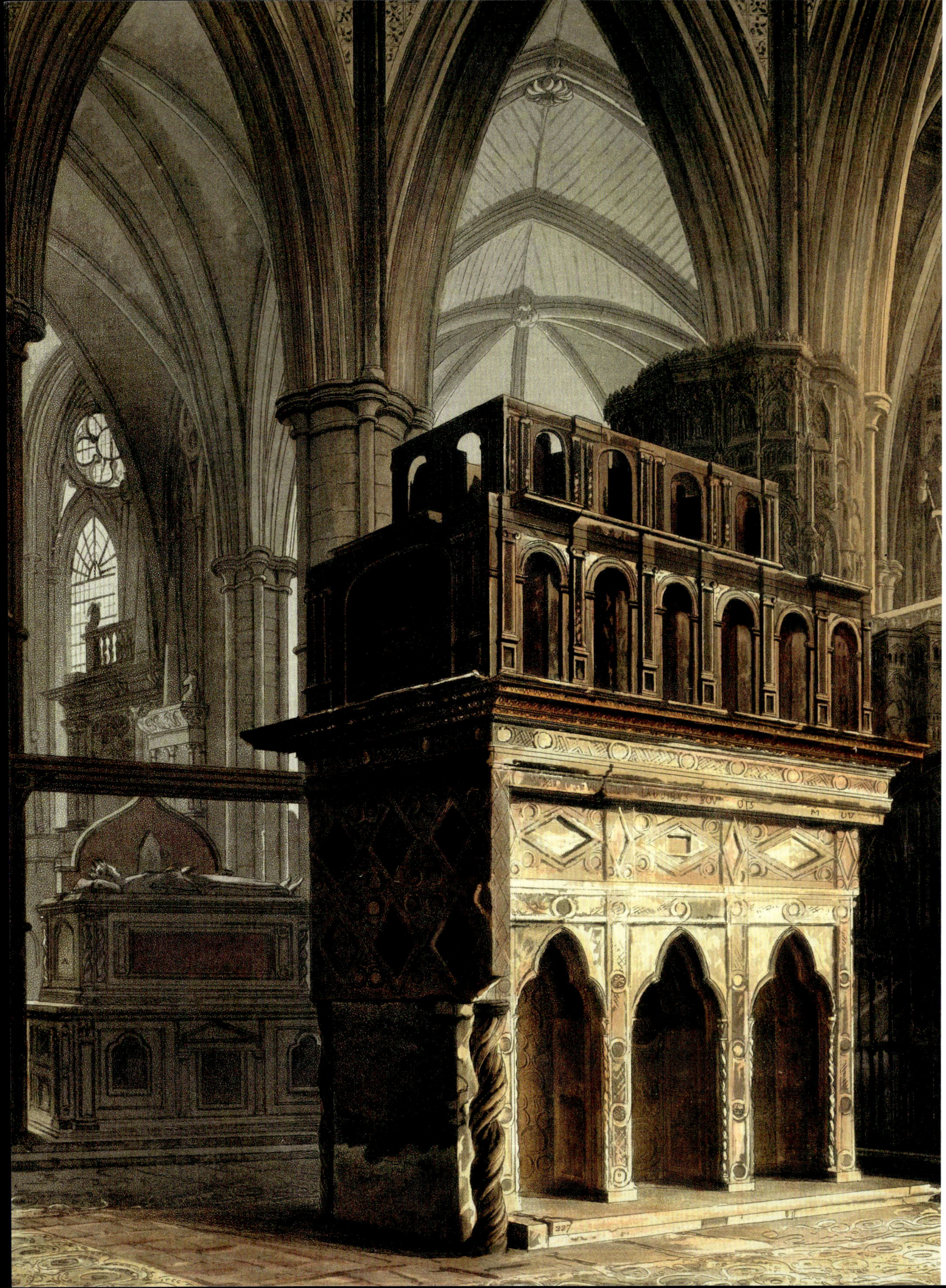

WESTMINSTER ABBEY'S close association with the monarchy stretches back almost 1000 years. When St Edward the Confessor embarked on rebuilding the church in the 1040s, he planned it as the site of his own eventual burial. On Christmas Day 1065, as the king's death approached, the formal consecration of the Abbey was rushed through. Edward died a week later and his burial site was to become the focus of royal devotion for many centuries, especially after he was recognised as a saint in 1161. This devotion was particularly strong in Henry III (1216–72), and was the motivation behind the wholesale rebuilding of the Abbey church overseen by him from 1245 until the new building's consecration on 13 October 1269 (although in fact much still remained unfinished).

ROYAL BURIALS

It was Henry III who probably first envisaged the Shrine of St Edward the Confessor, which was itself rebuilt in lavish style, as the centrepiece of a royal mausoleum. He chose for his own burial the most important location on the north side of the shrine, where his remains and effigy still lie. Gradually, over the next two centuries, Henry's successors as monarchs joined him, first in tombs surrounding the shrine and then, when that space was filled, in the Abbey's Lady Chapel, where Henry VII (1485–1509) was the first of 15 kings and queens to be buried, in 1509. This chapel was constructed from 1503 by Henry VII to replace its thirteenth-century version, initially with a view to relocating the body of Henry VI (1422–71) from Windsor but, when that was unsuccessful, as the burial place for himself and his wife.

In all, 13 British kings and four queens regnant are buried in the Abbey, along with a further 11 queens consort. In addition, numerous princes and princesses and other members of the royal family have been laid to rest within its walls. The last king to be buried here was George II in 1760, the last chapter in the Abbey's history of 700 years as a royal mausoleum. His successors have chosen Windsor as their resting place, although very often the funeral service has been

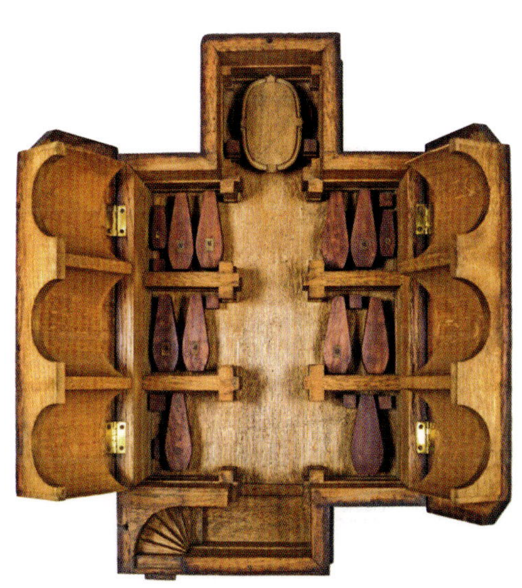

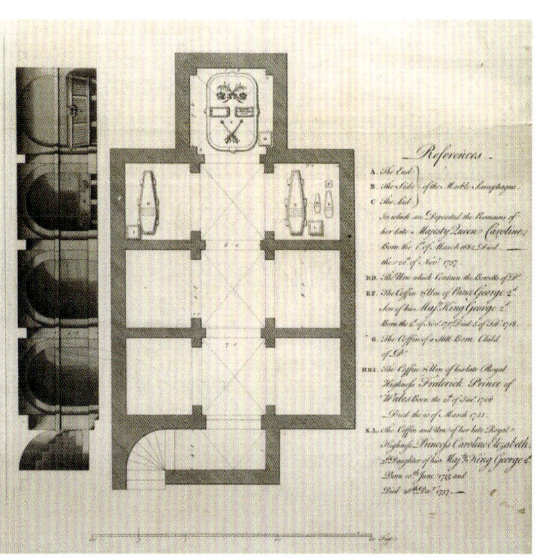

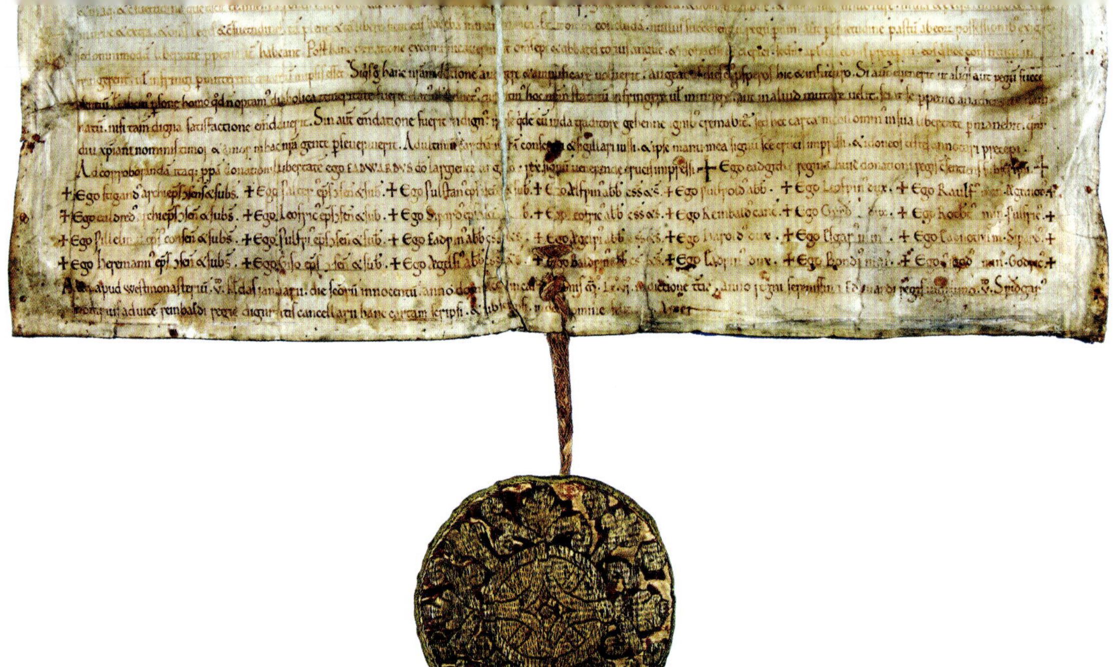

conducted at Westminster in acknowledgement of its special role. This was most recently the case for the funeral service for Queen Elizabeth the Queen Mother in 2002. In 1997 the funeral service of Diana, Princess of Wales was held in the Abbey, before her body was taken to be buried in Althorp Park in Northamptonshire.

Many of these monarchs are memorialised within the Abbey with impressive tombs and monumental effigies, some of the finest and most important works of art of their periods. Fashions change, however, and most of the later royal burials are marked only with discreet floor stones. In the medieval and early modern period, royal funerals included the use of wooden effigies, carried on top of the coffins, and of funerary achievements, symbols of knighthood displayed around the tomb. Many of these remained at the Abbey, and now form part of the collections on display.

CORONATIONS

St Edward the Confessor's choice of royal burial site also settled the question of the location for coronations in England. Until this point, several churches had provided the setting for the coronations of Anglo-Saxon monarchs, reflecting the divided nature of the early kingdoms. A number of kings were crowned at Kingston-upon-Thames

in the tenth century; the Confessor himself had been crowned at Winchester in 1042. We do not know for certain where St Edward the Confessor's immediate successor, Harold (1065–66), was crowned, but it was very probably at Westminster; proximity to the recently-deceased Edward would have lent legitimacy to his claim to the throne.

By the end of the same year, however, after Harold had been defeated at the battle of Hastings, it was to Westminster that the new king, William the Conqueror (1066–87), went for his coronation. On Christmas Day 1066 he launched a new Norman dynasty in the Confessor's royal church. Since that date, every monarch that has been crowned has had a coronation at Westminster Abbey. Two kings were never crowned: Edward V, who died in around 1483 aged only about 13, and Edward VIII, who abdicated in 1936 before the service could take place. Henry III, on the other hand, was crowned twice, first in October 1216 in Gloucester, immediately after his accession, to cement his claim to the throne (and because London was then in the hands of the rebel barons and their French backers). He staged a second, more formal and elaborate coronation at Westminster nearly four years later, when civil war had been ended. Westminster Abbey was already regarded as the coronation church, and only by undergoing the rituals and orders

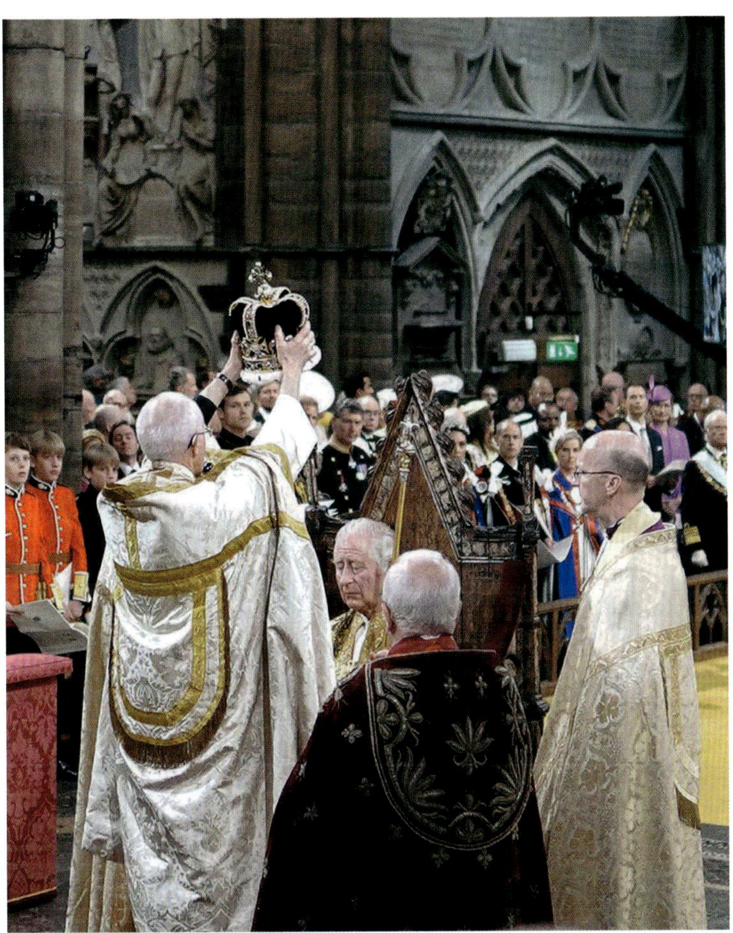

29 April 2011. In the twentieth century, the Abbey became the setting for a number of such royal occasions; until then, royal weddings had usually been private affairs, and it was only from the 1920s that they again became public events. The future Queen Elizabeth II married Lieutenant Philip Mountbatten RN at the Abbey in 1947, and two of her four children were also married here. Despite being personal occasions, these services have also become national events and are watched by record audiences around the globe.

OTHER ROYAL ASSOCIATIONS

The Abbey's exceptional status as a royal church was formally recognised in 1222, when the Archbishop of Canterbury acknowledged that it fell outside the jurisdiction of the Bishop of London, and was in fact answerable directly to the pope. In 1560 when Elizabeth I (1558–1603) formally re-established the Abbey as the Collegiate Church of St Peter, Westminster, this special status was reflected when the Abbey was made one of the few royal peculiars. These, which include St George's Chapel Windsor, the Chapels Royal and the chapels in the Tower of London, have a 'peculiar jurisdiction' of not being subject to the Bishop of London (or to the Archbishop of Canterbury) but instead being directly answerable to the sovereign. This status continues to this day.

Successive monarchs have lavished particular attention on the Abbey. In the medieval period, this included paying for the building of many parts of the church (notably the general rebuilding under Henry III, the reconstruction of the nave by Richard II, and the new Lady Chapel built by Henry VII); granting the Abbey extensive lands and privileges, to help maintain the number of monks to pray there, and to beautify the royal church; and attending services and national events within its walls. While the lands and most of the privileges (as well as the monks) have gone, this last tradition continues. The King and other members of the royal family attend numerous services at the Abbey each year, both annual special services such as the Commonwealth Service, the opening of the Field of Remembrance and the Battle of Britain service, and many individual services which play an important role in the collective act of worship and remembrance of the nation.

embodied in the religious service there would he be accepted as the legitimate monarch.

The coronation of His Majesty King Charles III and Queen Camilla on 6 May 2023 is the latest example of a 900-year-old tradition at the Abbey. The service for the king's mother, Her Majesty Queen Elizabeth II on 2 June 1953 had been the first to be televised and it changed the public's perception both of the Crown and of the royal family. In 2023, King Charles made several changes to update the ceremony which took place in an Abbey prepared to broadcast the coronation to many millions of people worldwide.

ROYAL WEDDINGS

Sixteen royal weddings are known to have taken place at Westminster Abbey, from that of Henry I to Princess Matilda of Scotland on 11 November 1100, to the wedding of His Royal Highness Prince William to Catherine Middleton on

I *Liber Regalis*, about 1382

The manuscript known as the *Liber Regalis*, or Royal Book, is, in effect, a manual for staging coronations and royal funerals. It was produced in about 1382 but it is not known for whom it was made. It is closely related to the Litlyngton Missal (see p.29), which was produced at a similar date. Both manuscripts contain the same orders for a coronation and the liturgy for royal funerals. The *Liber Regalis* was probably made locally to the Abbey, possibly using continental artists. It is not certainly known to have been at the Abbey until the late seventeenth century, though it probably arrived here a great deal earlier. Because of its usefulness for those charged with organising coronations, it may be one of the very few books left at the Abbey after the destruction and dispersal of the library at the dissolution of the monasteries in 1540. The ceremonial instructions and order of service contained in the manuscript reflect the service as it was performed until the reign of Elizabeth I. Indeed, despite various changes after that date, the basic format remains recognisable in all subsequent coronation services.

The manuscript is written on vellum (calfskin). It contains four illuminated images to illustrate the accompanying text: the act of crowning a king, a king and queen together, a queen alone, and the funeral of a king. In this image, the king and queen are crowned simultaneously, although the queen's throne sits on a lower step than that of the king. Anne of Bohemia, however, was crowned on her own in 1382; Richard II, her husband, in 1377. A century passed before the next joint coronation, that of Richard III and Anne Neville in 1483.

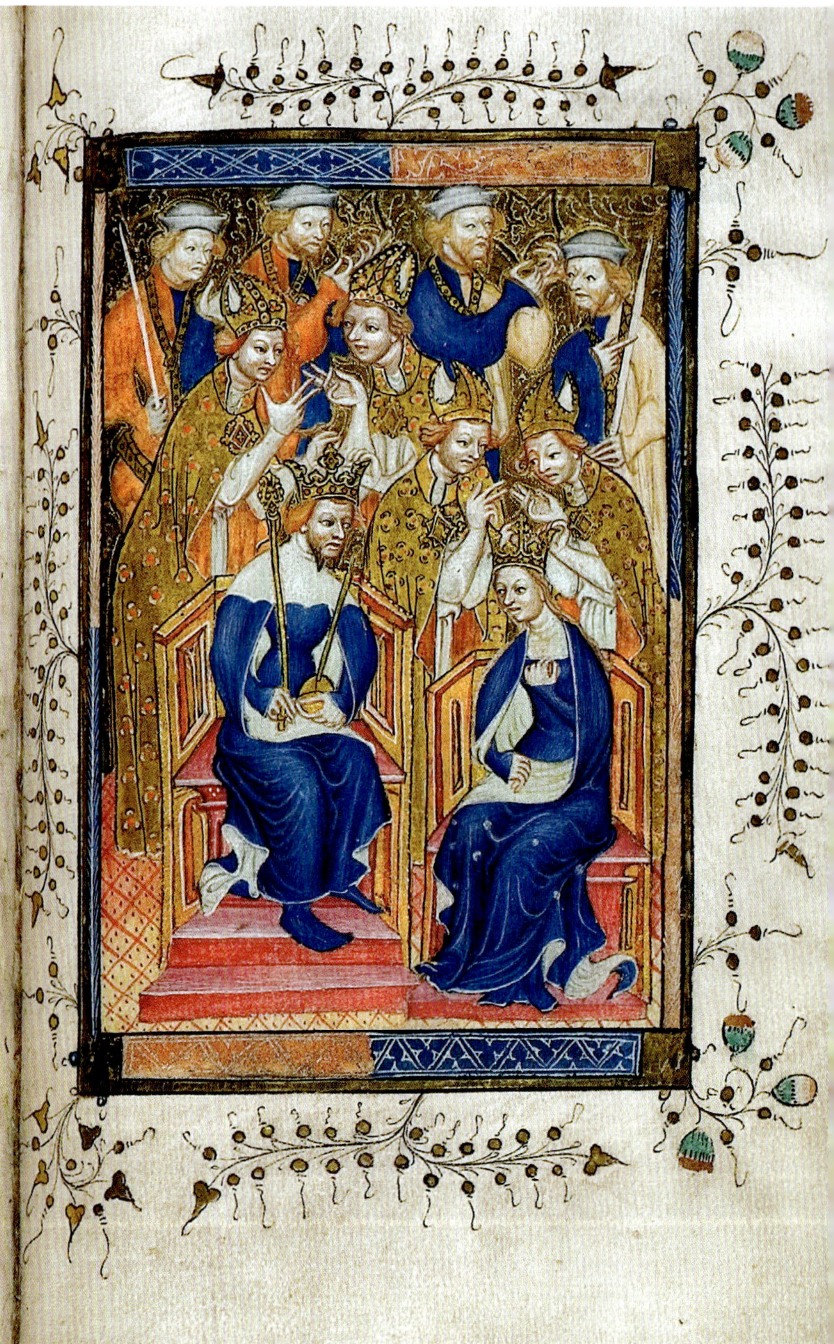

WAL MS 38

2 Replica Coronation Regalia, 1937

The coronation is a religious service and has always involved ritual and pageantry and the use of a variety of symbolic objects in the ceremony. Although we have relatively little information about the earliest coronations in England, which were those of Anglo-Saxon monarchs, some form of investiture with weapons and regalia was certainly practised. Crowns are depicted in early manuscripts from the tenth century onwards; St Edward the Confessor was crowned at Winchester in 1043, and is also shown bearing an orb and a rod. As the coronation ceremony became settled, other regalia gradually became incorporated: swords, staff, orb, sceptre, spurs, ampulla (small containers for holy oil), armills (a type of bracelet to be worn on the arm) and so on. These would be carried by nobles, both as signs of kingship and royal dignity, and as relics bestowing legitimacy on the ceremony. Many of these objects were traditionally stored at Westminster Abbey, but the current Crown Jewels have been housed at the Tower of London since the seventeenth century.

After the execution of Charles I in 1649 and the temporary end of monarchy in England, almost all of the medieval coronation regalia was destroyed or dispersed. When Charles II was restored to the throne in 1660, a new set had to be made for his coronation the following year. The items created at this date form the centrepieces of today's Crown Jewels. The regalia on display in The Queen's Diamond Jubilee Galleries are replicas made for George VI's coronation in 1937 by the London firm of Messrs Robert White and Sons, to be used for rehearsals and then for display. After its use in the preparations for Queen Elizabeth II's coronation in 1953, this replica set was purchased jointly by the Abbey and the Ministry of Works and has been kept at the Abbey ever since. The larger crown is a replica of St Edward's Crown, named after St Edward the Confessor, which is used for the actual crowning of the sovereign. The original was made in 1661 and has 444 semi-precious stones set in a solid gold frame, possibly remodelled from an earlier crown. At the end of the coronation service the monarch puts on the lighter Imperial State Crown for the procession out of the Abbey.

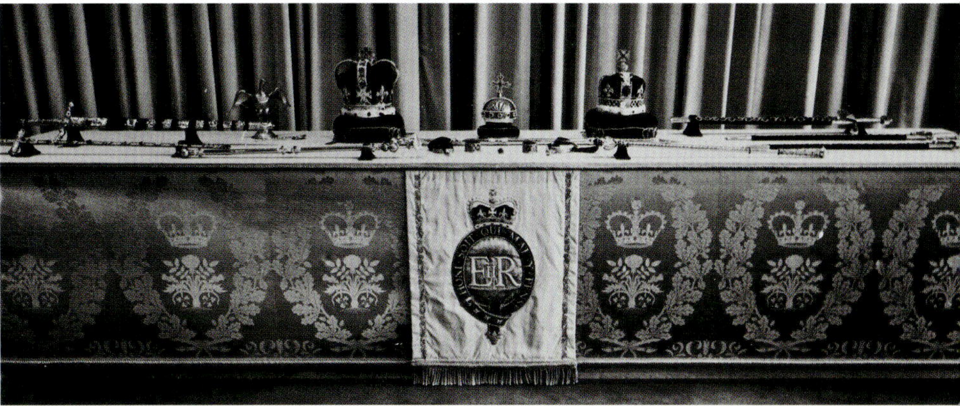

Replica Regalia laid out on the Regalia table in the Coronation Annexe in 1953 (from a set of souvenir photographs)

Replica orb. The cross symbolises Christ's sovereignty over the Earth

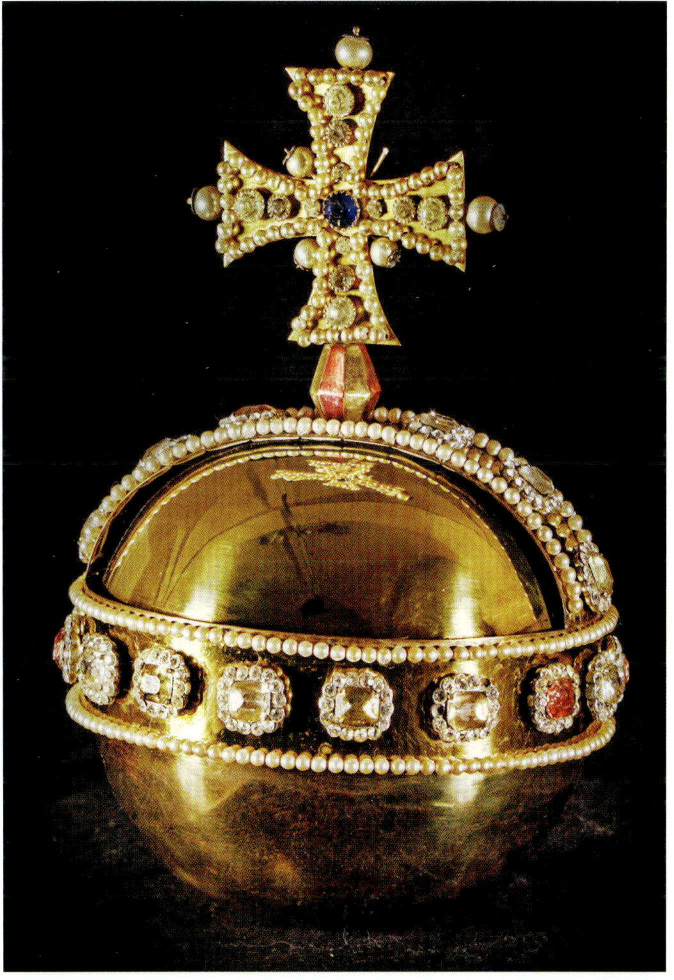

WA 0854

41

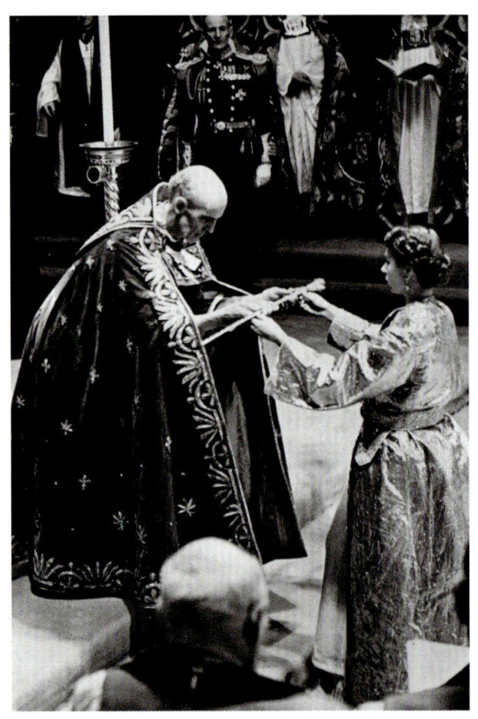

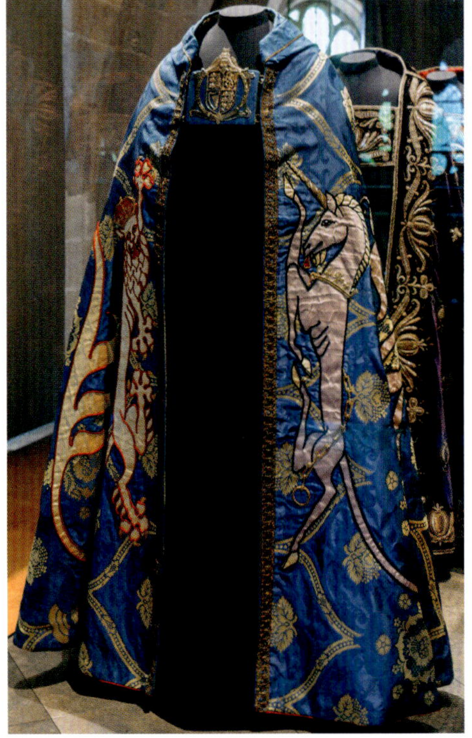

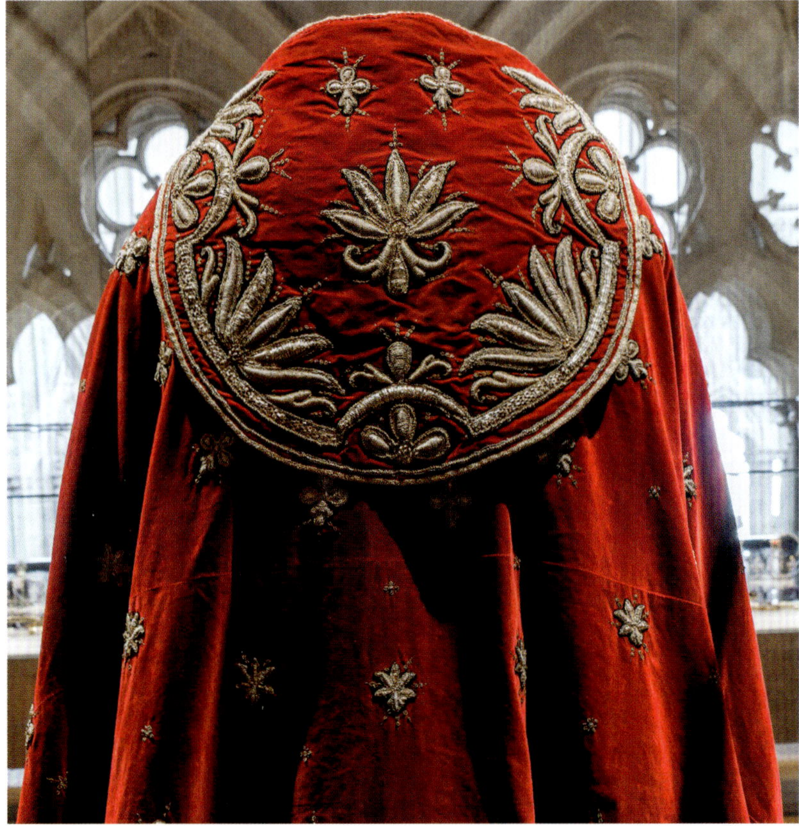

3 Coronation Copes

Vestments (distinctive forms of clothing) have been worn by ecclesiastical figures since the very early days of the Church. As the liturgy became more established, so too did the types of clothing required for each form of service. In the middle ages, the chasuble was the main vestment worn by priests serving at the Eucharist; at the daily and special services, the garment worn was the cope, a decorated cloak fastened at the neck and extending to the ankles. The use of vestments declined generally in the sixteenth and seventeenth centuries but they continued in use at Westminster Abbey, primarily for great state occasions. Traditionally a new monarch makes a gift of the fabric for new copes to be worn at their coronation. The Abbey therefore has an important collection of historic copes, made for and worn by successive deans and canons over the last three centuries.

In 1953 new blue and gold floral silk copes (left) were made for the coronation of Her Majesty Queen Elizabeth II by clerical outfitters Watts & Co and to a design by Keith Murray, bearing a lion and a unicorn, the heraldic supporters on the royal coat of arms. In the event, Dean Don did not wear this cope for the service but chose instead to wear the oldest cope in the Abbey collection (above left and centre), which had been made for the coronation of Charles II in 1661, from crimson velvet decorated with five-petalled flowers and stars. His successor, Dean Hoyle, made the same choice in 2023.

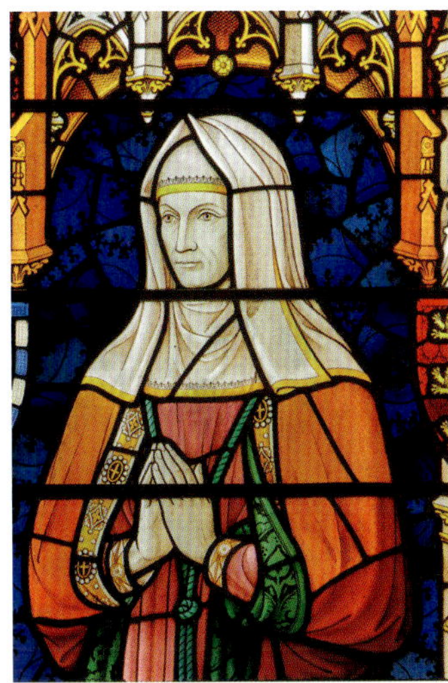

Lady Margaret Beaufort (1443–1509) was the mother of King Henry VII and one of the founders of the new Tudor dynasty. Her long and close association with Westminster Abbey began as early as 1496, when she endowed daily prayers to be said for her by the monks. In 1505 she established a chantry chapel at the Abbey, which funded monks to pray for her while she was alive, and for her soul once she was dead. After the death of her son in April 1509 and until the coronation of her grandson, Henry VIII, two months later, Lady Margaret lodged in part of Abbot Islip's house, now part of the Deanery. She died there five days after the coronation and was buried in the chapel built for her on the south side of the new Lady Chapel, where a magnificent effigy by Pietro Torrigiano was placed over her tomb.

This small private prayer book, in Latin and English, dates from about 1500 and was probably inherited by Lady Margaret from her fourth husband, Thomas Stanley, who died in 1504. She may well have used it while staying at the Abbey, although the manuscript was only given to the Abbey in the twentieth century. The illumination (right) shows the New Testament scene of the crucifixion (elsewhere it bears the Beaufort, later Tudor, badge of a portcullis in the initial, and red Tudor roses in the border). The manuscript was almost certainly produced in England, possibly by the Dutch artist (or studio) known as the Master of the Dark Eyes, who was at work in London at the time.

Other objects associated with Lady Margaret Beaufort are also on display in the new Galleries. These include a travelling chest, which she reputedly left at the Abbey at her death. This is displayed beneath a stained glass window (above left) depicting her alongside Eleanor of Castile (1241–90), wife of Edward I, who is also buried in the Abbey. The windows were designed by Sir John Ninian Comper in 1951.

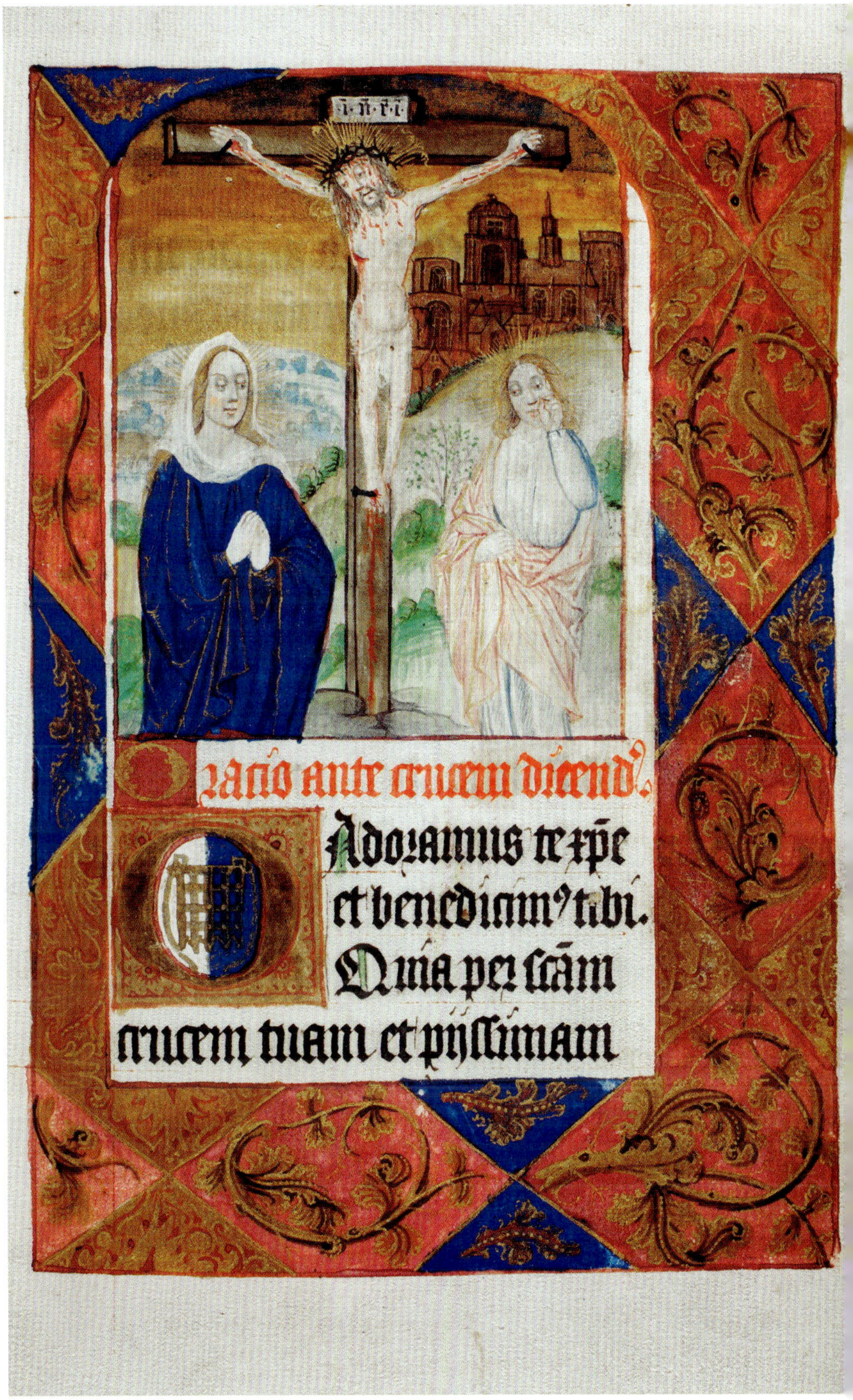

WAL MS 39

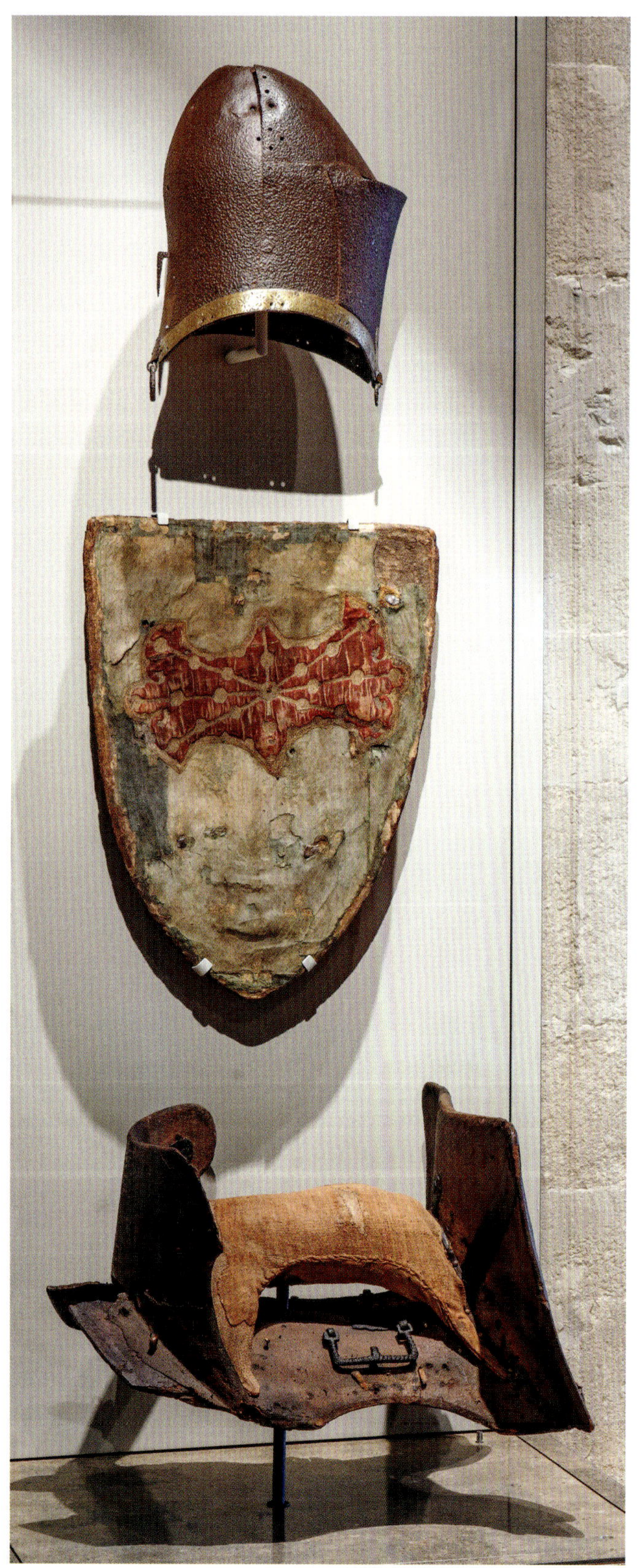

5 Funeral achievements associated with Henry V, 1422

In the later middle ages it was traditional for the funeral processions of kings, nobles and other major figures to include a set of funeral achievements, an armorial display of objects associated with the chivalric knight. These objects might include helmets, gauntlets, shields and banners, and equipment for horses. After the funeral, they were displayed over the tomb and often remained in the church where the funeral service was held.

This great helm (helmet) is believed to have formed part of the funeral achievements of Henry V (1413–22), who was buried at Westminster Abbey on 7 November 1422. Other parts of his achievements to survive include a shield and a saddle. The shield, the front of which would originally have displayed the royal arms of England and France, has on its back a crimson velvet armband, embroidered with the arms of Joan of Navarre. Henry V was her stepson, suggesting that the shield may originally have belonged to his father, Henry IV. The saddle is the earliest surviving example of a new lightweight form, and was originally covered in blue velvet with a fleur-de-lis pattern. A sword, also supposedly part of the achievements, was actually made about 100 years later, possibly in Italy. The sword was discovered in the triforium of the Abbey in 1869.

The helm is constructed of five sections, with reinforced plates at the front, suggesting that it was originally designed for use in tournaments. It was made in England, probably in London, from iron and copper alloy, and contains holes on top where a crest would have been attached. If it was included in Henry V's funeral, the crest would have depicted a heraldic leopard to represent England.

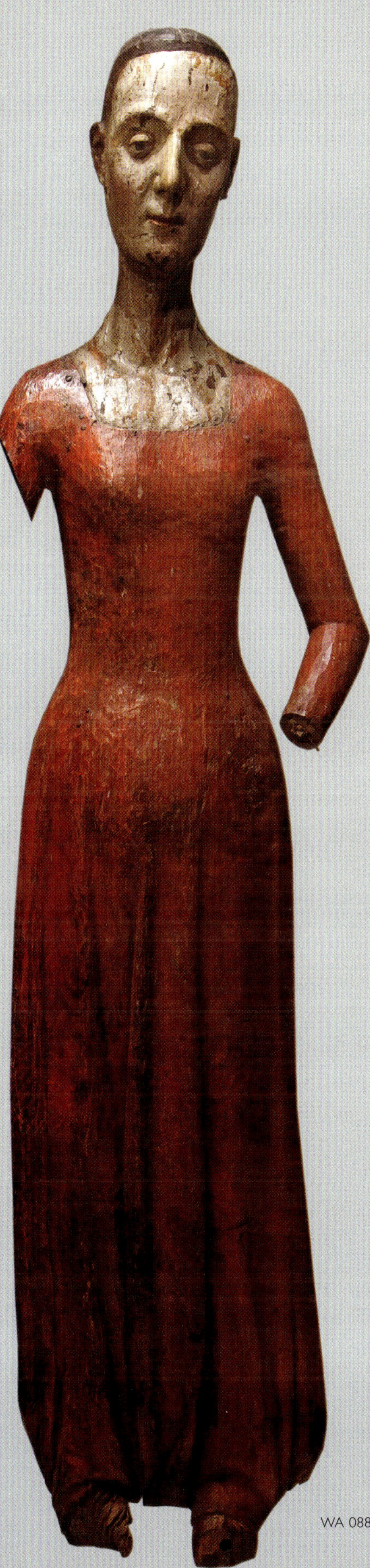

6 Funeral effigy of Catherine de Valois, 1437

From the fourteenth until the early seventeenth centuries, royal funerals included an effigy of the deceased monarch as part of the procession of the coffin to the church. This lay on top of the coffin, representing the individual to those attending the funeral. The first recorded instance was for the burial of Edward II at Gloucester Abbey in 1327, and from 1377, the funeral of Edward III, until that of James I in 1625, the practice was followed for the majority of royal funerals at Westminster Abbey. After the service, the effigies were usually left at the Abbey, forming a collection of royal effigies of which a large number survive. Some have been heavily damaged in the intervening years, but many remain remarkable pieces of sculpture in their own right.

The remains of the effigy of Catherine de Valois (1401–37), wife of Henry V, are carved from a single piece of wood. Separate sections would have been used to make the missing right arm, and the hands. No other authentic portrait of the queen survives, so her effigy provides our closest depiction of her. Although she is portrayed clothed, the effigy would have been covered in real garments for the funeral, with a wig, and possibly a crown, on the head.

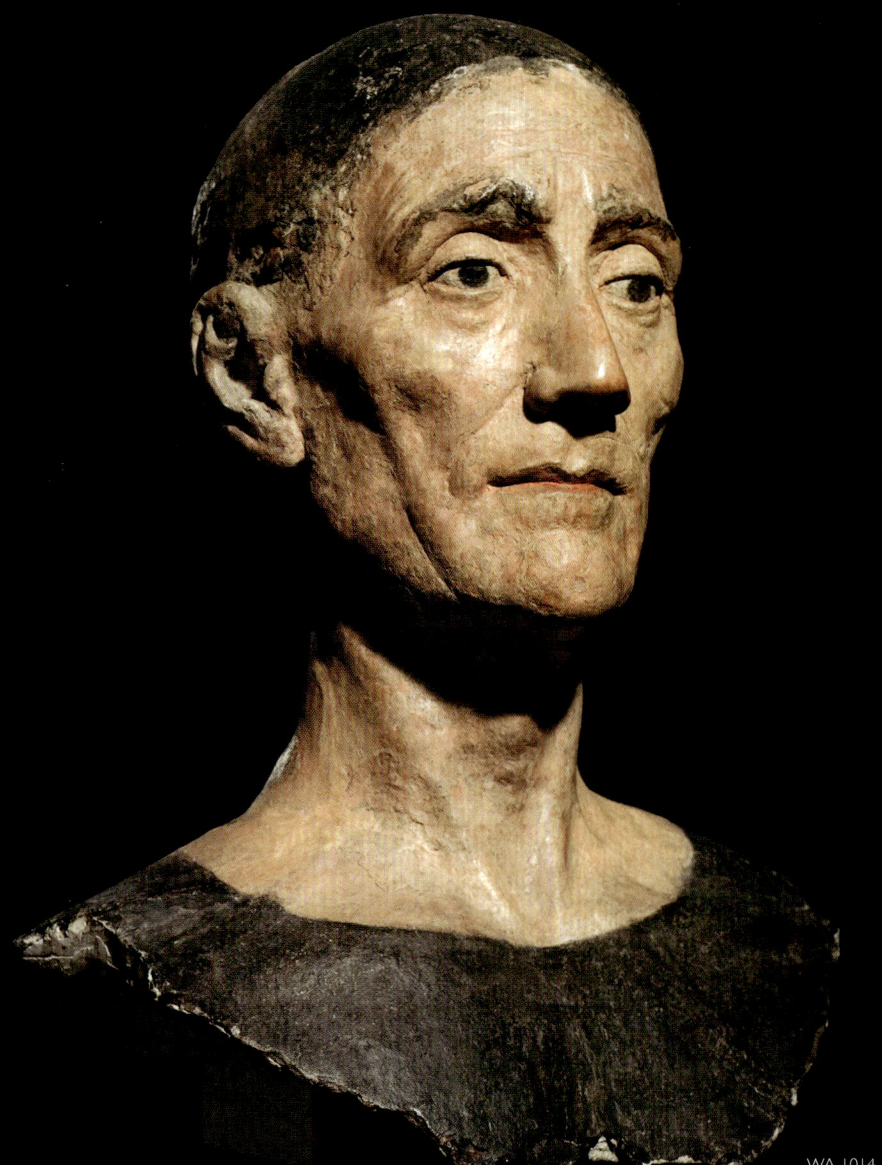

7 Funeral effigy head of Henry VII, 1509

The features of royal funeral effigies were sometimes modelled on death masks and can therefore offer accurate representations of these major historical figures. The head of Henry VII (1485–1509) is one of the finest of those to survive. It is more lifelike than any of its predecessors (and, indeed, most of those which came after), reflecting the growing sophistication of royal portraiture in Renaissance England. It is probably the work of the Italian artist Pietro Torrigiano (1472–1528), who was also responsible for the king's tomb and for a remarkable terracotta portrait bust of the king, now in the Victoria and Albert Museum. There are close parallels between all these portraits. The clothing which would have adorned the effigy, the king's parliamentary robes, had been lost by 1907, and much of the body was destroyed in the Second World War.

Effigies continued to be used in funeral processions until the seventeenth century. No funeral was held in 1649 for the executed King Charles I, however, and from this time effigies were never again used in royal funeral observances. After the Restoration in 1660, effigies were again produced but for other reasons, either in continuation of the series, or purchased by the Abbey as tourist attractions.

The only occasion in English history on which two monarchs have been crowned joint rulers was the coronation of William III and Mary II in 1689. Mary was monarch in her own right, as daughter of James II, and not just as queen consort (that is, wife of the king). Both William and Mary were offered the crown in February 1689, after the deposition of James II in 1688, and their coronation took place two months later. A second coronation chair was therefore required, to complement the ancient chair constructed in the reign of Edward I nearly 400 years before (below right, and on display in St George's Chapel in the Abbey). In the end, Mary occupied this chair, although her claim to the throne was stronger than her husband's.

The new chair was modelled on its historic counterpart but with substantially less decoration, and was probably made in the workshop of Thomas Roberts, Joiner to the Great Wardrobe. The chair may have been used once or twice subsequently for queens consort, for example at the coronation of William IV and Queen Adelaide in 1831. It has been carved with the initials of many visitors to the Abbey, mainly in the eighteenth century and traditionally including a number of Westminster schoolboys. The wood for the chair seems to have been brought from the Netherlands, and the main panels come from a single oak tree.

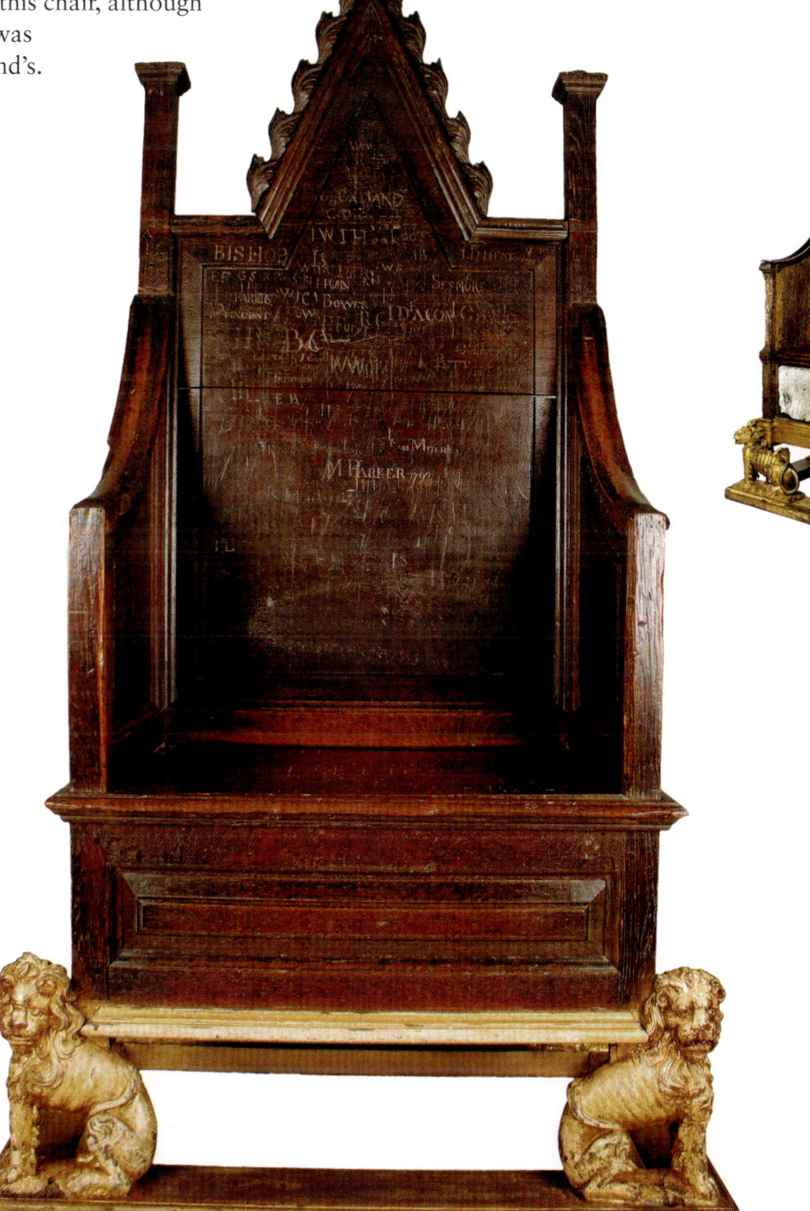

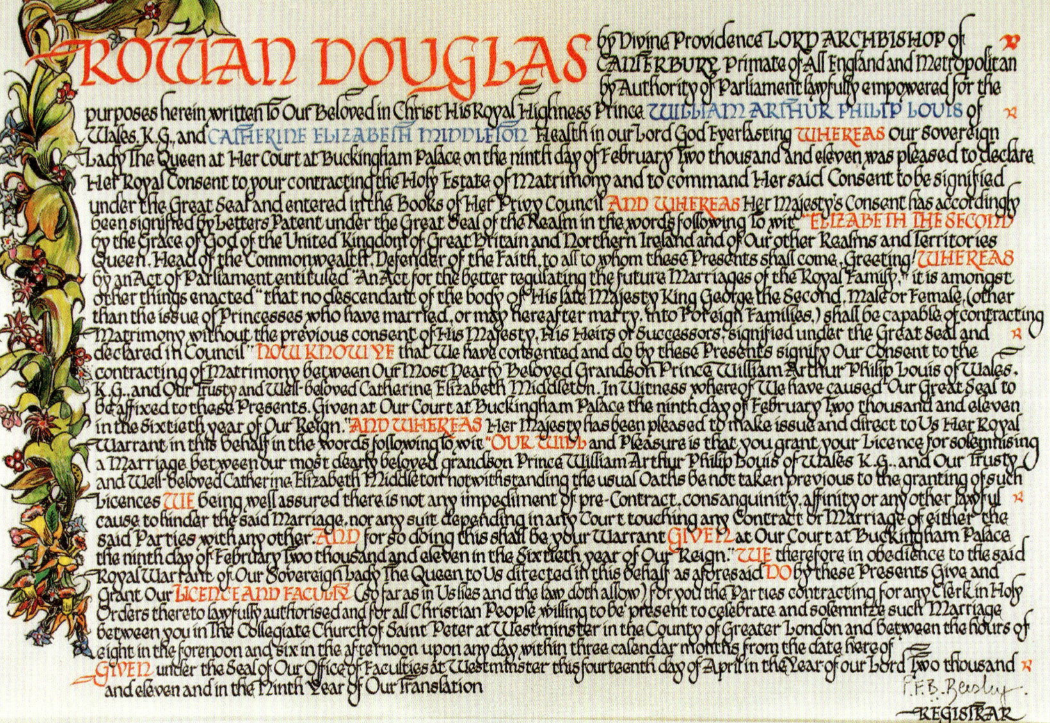

WAM CIX

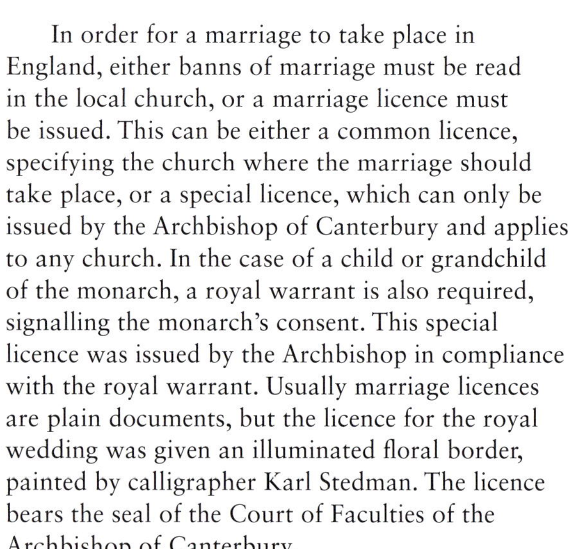

9 Marriage licence of HRH Prince William and Miss Catherine Middleton, 2011

Westminster Abbey has been the location for royal weddings for almost as long as for coronations. The first recorded royal wedding held at the Abbey was that of Henry I to Princess Matilda of Scotland, on 11 November 1100, and the tradition continues in the twenty-first century. The marriage of Prince William, son of King Charles III, to Catherine Middleton took place in Westminster Abbey on 29 April 2011 and was watched on television by an estimated nearly two and a half billion people worldwide. The service was conducted by the Dean of Westminster, the Very Reverend Dr John Hall, and the marriage was solemnised by the Archbishop of Canterbury, the Most Reverend and Right Honourable Dr Rowan Williams.

In order for a marriage to take place in England, either banns of marriage must be read in the local church, or a marriage licence must be issued. This can be either a common licence, specifying the church where the marriage should take place, or a special licence, which can only be issued by the Archbishop of Canterbury and applies to any church. In the case of a child or grandchild of the monarch, a royal warrant is also required, signalling the monarch's consent. This special licence was issued by the Archbishop in compliance with the royal warrant. Usually marriage licences are plain documents, but the licence for the royal wedding was given an illuminated floral border, painted by calligrapher Karl Stedman. The licence bears the seal of the Court of Faculties of the Archbishop of Canterbury.

This portrait of Queen Elizabeth II was painted by the Australian artist Ralph Heimans to commemorate The Queen's Diamond Jubilee in 2012. In an imagined scene, she is depicted in her State dress, standing 'in a moment of quiet reflection' on the spot on the Cosmati pavement where she was crowned 60 years earlier. In 2015, Queen Elizabeth became Britain's longest-serving monarch, surpassing the reign of her great-great-grandmother, Queen Victoria, who reigned from 1837 to 1901. She died in 2022 and was succeeded by her son, King Charles III. The portrait was purchased for the Abbey by Lord and Lady Harris of Peckham in 2013, to mark the anniversary of the coronation at the Abbey on 2 June 1953.

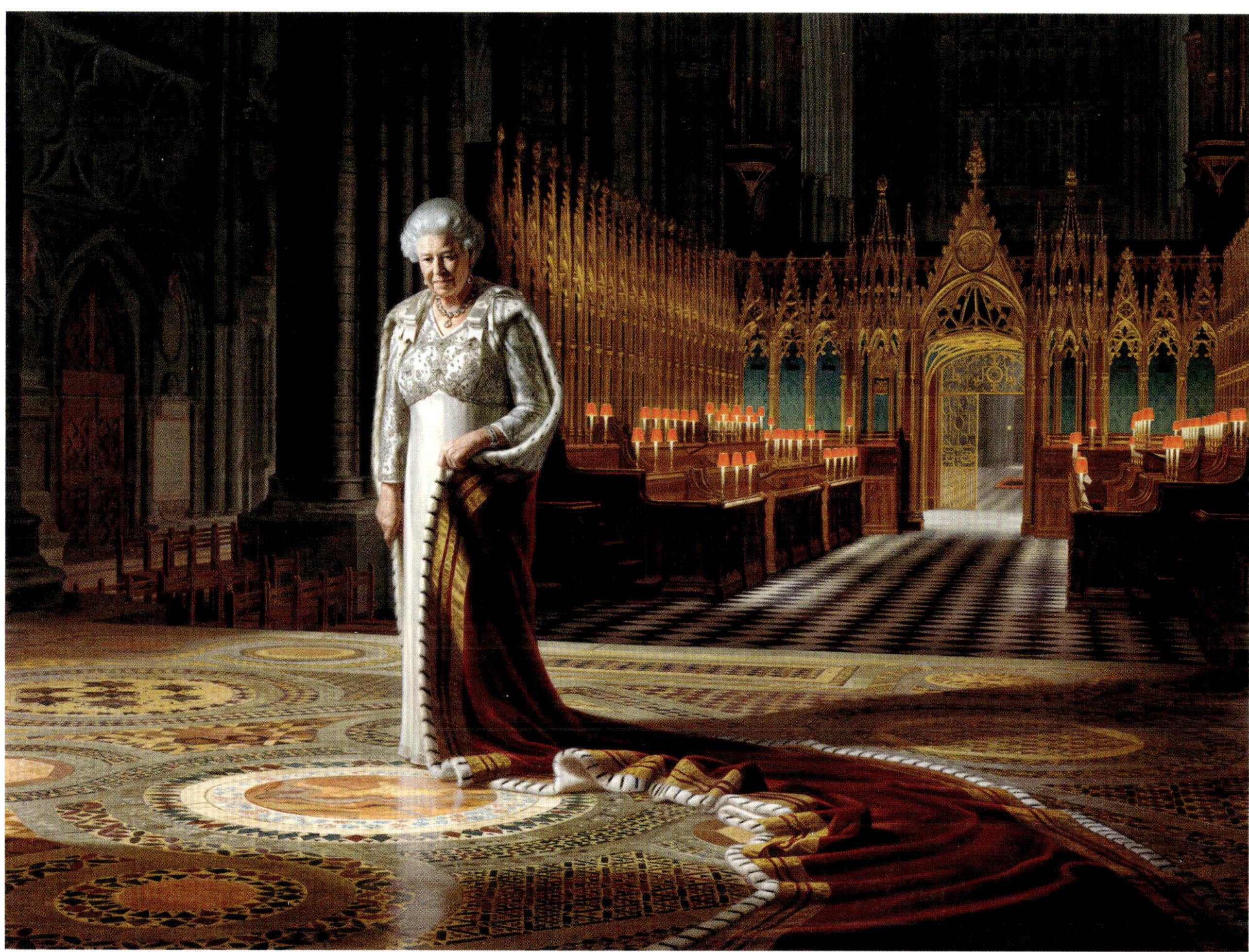

WA 3151

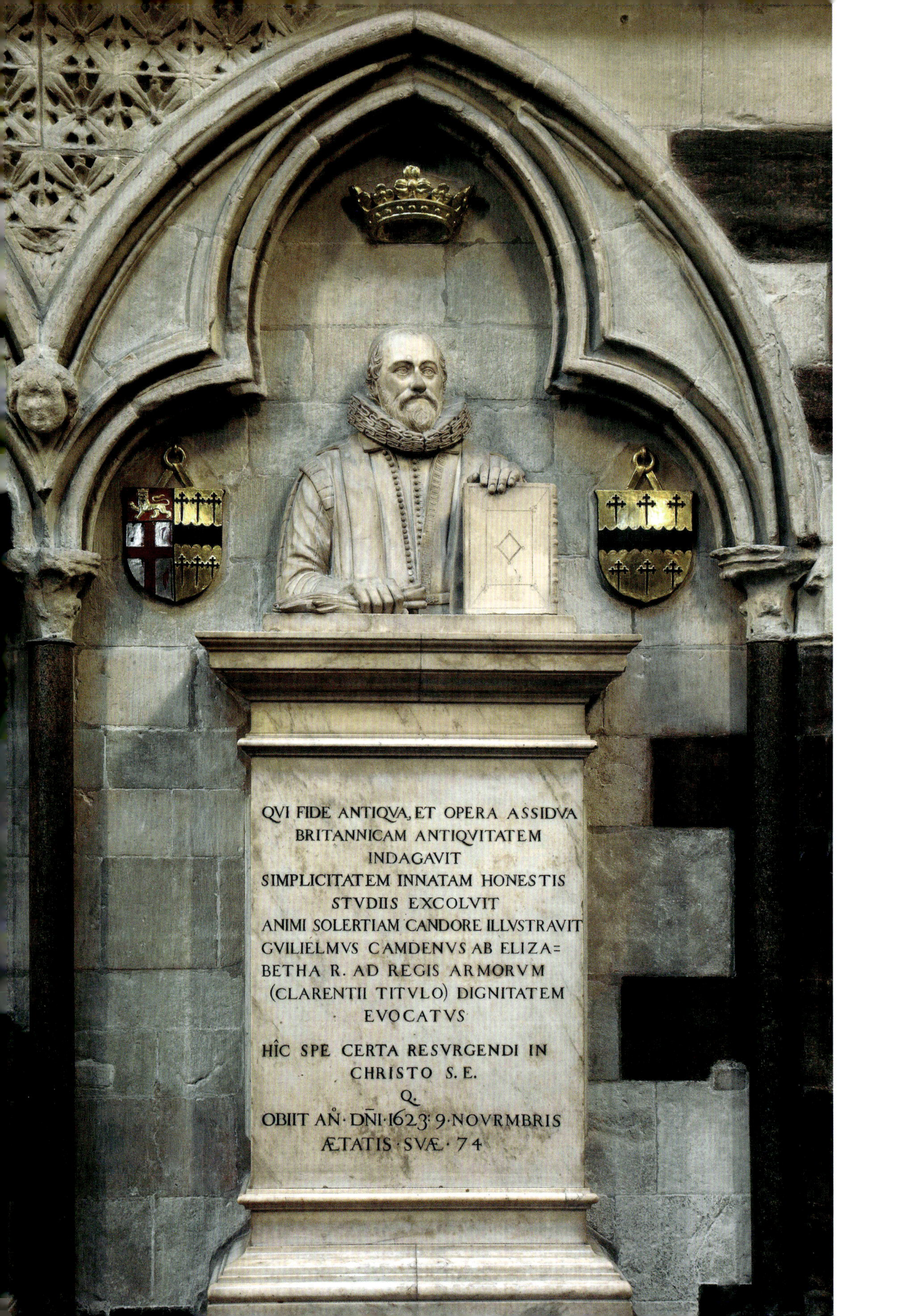

QVI FIDE ANTIQVA, ET OPERA ASSIDVA
BRITANNICAM ANTIQVITATEM
INDAGAVIT
SIMPLICITATEM INNATAM HONESTIS
STVDIIS EXCOLVIT
ANIMI SOLERTIAM CANDORE ILLVSTRAVIT
GVILIELMVS CAMDENVS AB ELIZA=
BETHA R. AD REGIS ARMORVM
(CLARENTII TITVLO) DIGNITATEM
EVOCATVS

HÎC SPE CERTA RESVRGENDI IN
CHRISTO S.E.
Q.
OBIIT AN· DÑI·1623: 9·NOVRMBRIS
ÆTATIS·SVÆ·74

WESTMINSTER ABBEY contains the most significant collection of monumental sculpture assembled in one place in the UK, its monuments and memorials reflecting the Abbey's particular role as a place of commemoration and remembrance. Important personalities in the history of the nation are buried or memorialised in the Abbey, and occasions of national significance are also observed here. Yet this aspect of the Abbey's life was never deliberately planned. Although some 3,000 people have been buried in Westminster Abbey since its foundation in the tenth century, the great majority of those burials have happened since the dissolution of the monastery in 1540. Throughout the middle ages the monks of Westminster carefully guarded the privilege of burial in their church. The erection of a tomb was a still greater honour.

With a few exceptions the Abbey's medieval tombs are the resting places of monarchs (around the Shrine of St Edward the Confessor), of Abbots of Westminster, and of a small number of nobles who had given service to the Crown or the Abbey. Apart from three examples on the north side of the sanctuary, the tombs of medieval aristocrats who were permitted to be buried in the Abbey are mostly in the chapels around the ambulatory, where they were positioned so as not to prevent the continued use of the chapels for worship. With the death of Henry VII royal burials moved into the new Lady Chapel, which became a mausoleum for the Tudor dynasty, although only the tombs of the founder and his mother, Lady Margaret Beaufort, were in place there prior to 1540.

Only after the dissolution of the monastery did a wider variety of tombs appear, especially in the ambulatory chapels which had lost their altars and now offered additional space. Elsewhere monuments appeared more slowly.

The nave remained empty of memorials until the 1630s and the north transept until the 1670s. In the south transept, however, the story was a different one. In 1556, during the revival of the Benedictine monastery under Mary I, the remains of the poet Geoffrey Chaucer (d. 1400) were moved from the original grave in St Benedict's Chapel to a new tomb in the south transept. Chaucer had been buried in the Abbey because he was clerk of works at the Palace of Westminster, and perhaps also because he lived in the monastery precinct. The re-burial was instigated by a minor poet called Nicholas Brigham, although his reasons for doing so are obscure. The appearance of a prominent tomb to Chaucer seems to have prompted the burial of the poet Edmund Spenser nearby in 1599, and the erection of his monument in 1620. By 1700 other literary figures had joined Chaucer and Spenser in the south transept, notably Beaumont, Drayton, Cowley and Dryden. In 1711 Joseph Addison (himself later memorialised in the south transept) referred in an essay to the Abbey's 'poetical quarter', while a published poem of 1733, 'Upon the Poets' Corner in Westminster Abbey', is the first known use of a title which has been applied to this part of the Abbey ever since. By the 1730s the absence of a memorial to William Shakespeare was seen as a significant lack, and the eventual erection of his monument in 1740, funded by public donations, confirms that the Abbey was now seen as the natural place to commemorate national personalities.

Around 40 writers are buried in the south transept while some 70 who are not buried at Westminster (or in a few cases who lie in other parts of the Abbey) are memorialised there. The styles of the memorials range from elaborate sculptures and near life-size statues to more modest floor stones. This same variety is found throughout the Abbey, and the quantity of memorials can seem overwhelming to the visitor. Just over 600 tombs and other substantial

Monument in the south transept to William Camden. He compiled the first guide to the Abbey's monuments

monuments, and more than 300 memorial stones and stained glass windows commemorate the achievements of scientists, musicians, politicians, philanthropists and many others. Not everyone commemorated in the Abbey would now be thought worthy of it. Some made their fortunes from the transatlantic slave trade, while others oversaw repressive or violent actions during British colonial rule abroad. Concern in the nineteenth century about the overcrowding of monuments was the reason for Parliament's decision to bury Lord Nelson at St Paul's Cathedral rather than the Abbey, and a number of monuments were subsequently taken up to the triforium. Others were reduced in size, but the belief that the Abbey was 'full' led to more radical proposals for new buildings in which to erect future memorials, and into which some existing memorials might be transferred.

Nothing came of these plans, partly because of the cost, but also because of an abiding national attachment to the Abbey as a special place of commemoration. In the end, space has always been found for new memorials when required, and the tradition continues to this day. The decision as to who may be buried or receive a memorial in the Abbey rests with the Dean of Westminster, but burials in the Abbey (and then only of cremated remains) are very rare.

To these traditions must be added the Abbey's unique series of funeral effigies, created originally for use in medieval royal funeral processions. Although this usage died out after the funeral of James I in 1625, it continued for a while at some non-royal funerals and the effigy remained an important memorial figure, to be placed beside the grave. By the nineteenth century the condition of many of the effigies had badly deteriorated and they were kept in a number of different places over the years, but the 'ragged regiment', as they were often called, continued to fascinate visitors and they are described in most of the early guidebooks to the Abbey.

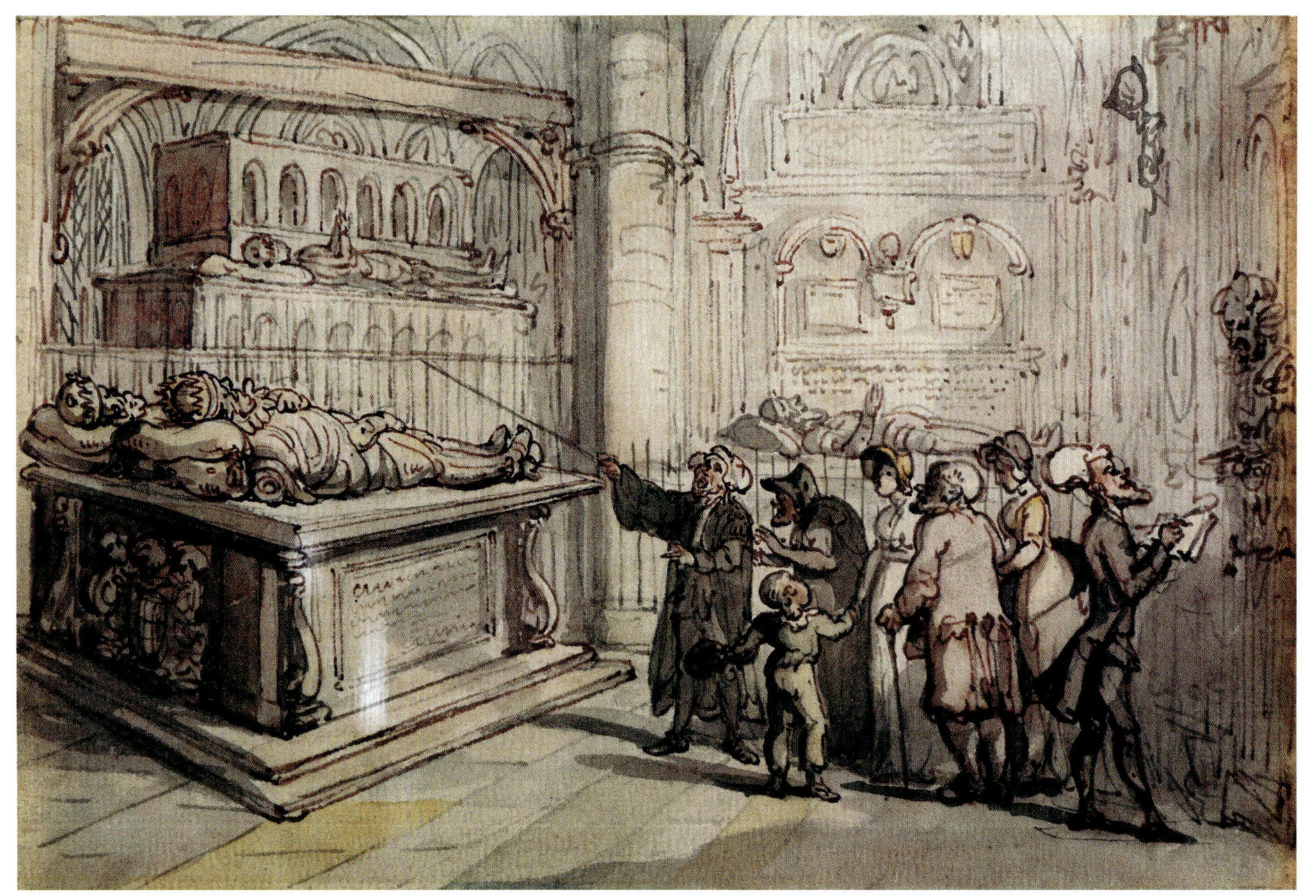

Ink and watercolour sketch by Thomas Rowlandson of visitors to Westminster Abbey, about 1810

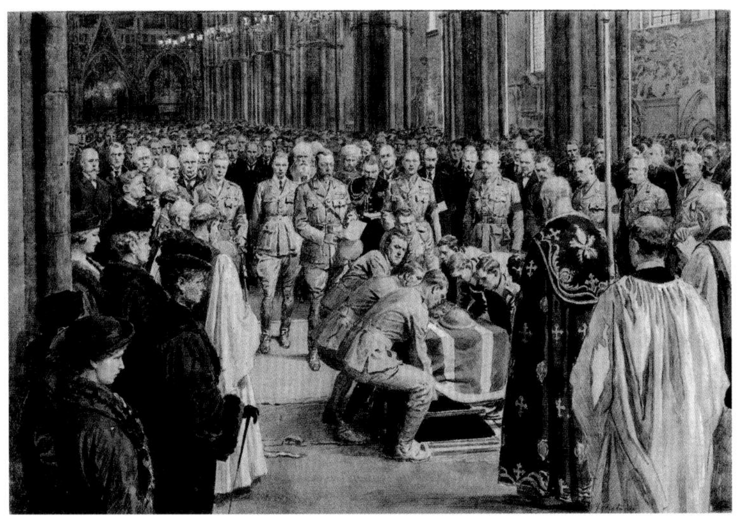

The First World War and its aftermath had a significant impact on Westminster Abbey as a place of memorialisation. Even before the end of the war in 1918, the Abbey had held special services of remembrance for those who had died but the burial of the Unknown Warrior at the west end of the nave, on 11 November 1920, provided a unique and abiding focus for remembrance within the church. The grave captured the public imagination and had particular significance for people grieving for those who had no known place of burial. The Grave of the Unknown Warrior, with its frame of Flanders poppies, is the particular focus of remembrance services and ceremonies every November, but wreaths are laid there throughout the year, especially by visiting heads of state, who come to the Abbey to pay their respects. Remembrance of war, and the need to work and pray for peace, is also reflected in the annual Field of Remembrance held beside the Abbey in St Margaret's Churchyard each November. The ground is divided into special plots, in which crosses adorned with poppies can be laid by the public to commemorate family and friends who have lost their lives in the two world wars, and also in more recent military conflicts.

The Abbey's impressive architecture, combined with its monuments and its many historic associations, have long made it a popular place to visit. Charges to visit various parts of the church were made from at least 1661 onwards, with the Abbey's vergers and 'tomb showers' leading early equivalents of guided tours. In 1697 a fee of threepence was being charged to visit all parts of the church, which had risen to sixpence by 1723. In the eighteenth century a visit to the Abbey was part of the fashionable itinerary for visitors to the capital. New monuments were described and critically assessed in the newspapers, encouraging public interest. A watercolour by the cartoonist Thomas Rowlandson, dated 1810, gently satirises a group of visitors to one of the chapels. Although most of the group listen as the guide discusses a particular tomb, one individual prefers to take notes on a different monument instead. In 1840 the Abbey received 37,465 visitors and two years later this number had risen to 51,444. Today more than a million visitors come to the Abbey every year.

The popularity of visiting the Abbey went hand in hand with the publication of guides and history books about the building. Early works, like William Camden's Latin account of the tombs, were soon supplemented by more accessible books in English describing the monuments and burials. By the eighteenth century there was considerable antiquarian interest in the Abbey's architecture and medieval remains, although treasures like the Westminster Retable, which now began to be discussed by historians, had been treated with little respect in the intervening centuries. John Dart's view, expressed in the introduction to his *Westmonasterium*, that no other church has so many notable burials and that the visitor is led 'to contemplate those glorious British heroes, to whose lasting Honour most of these monuments were erected', shows the degree to which the Abbey's place as a repository of national memory was already well established by 1723. This perception was further reinforced in Victorian times by Dean Arthur Penrhyn Stanley, who supported the continued burial and memorialisation of important individuals such as David Livingstone and Charles Dickens. A model of an unexecuted design for Stanley's own memorial is displayed in the Galleries. In his influential book *Memorials of Westminster Abbey* (first published in 1868 and reprinted in many subsequent editions), Stanley used the tombs and monuments to show how the Abbey's and the nation's histories were intertwined, a relationship which continues to fascinate to this day.

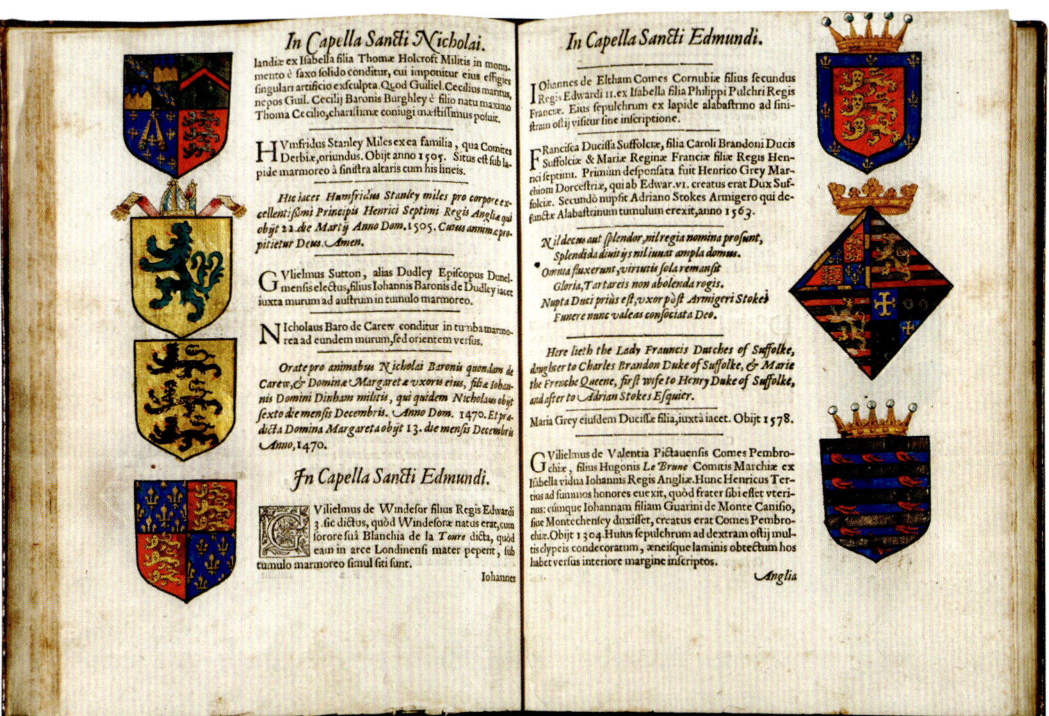

William Camden's own copy of his guide to the Abbey's monuments (top) and the miniature guide in the 'Gigantick Histories' series by Thomas Boreman

| Three early guidebooks: *The Kings, Queens, Nobles and Others buried in the Collegiate Church of Blessed Peter at Westminster, 1600; Westmonasterium. Or The History and Antiquities of the Abbey Church of St. Peter's Westminster, 1723; The 'Gigantick History' of Westminster Abbey, 1742*

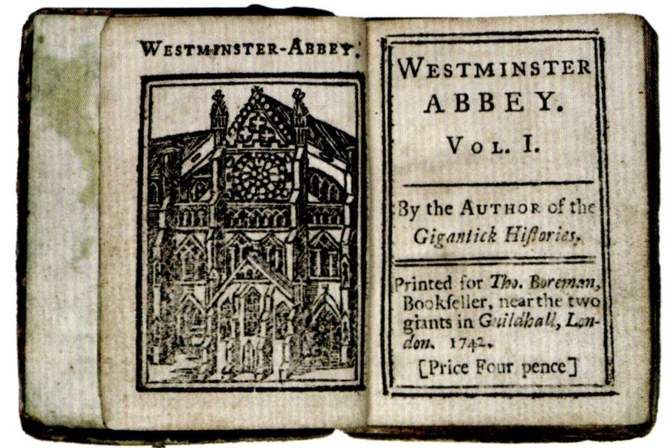

These volumes show how the Abbey's buildings and their contents began to be recorded in print. William Camden was an important historian of ancient Britain and, from 1587, the Abbey's first librarian. Motivated by a desire to record the country's medieval past, he published this account of the Abbey's tombs. Although it is written entirely in Latin, it can reasonably claim to be the earliest published guide to the Abbey and records some inscriptions which no longer survive. The displayed copy is decorated with hand-coloured coats of arms matching those on the tombs being described, and it seems likely that this was Camden's own copy.

John Dart's *Westmonasterium* stands in the line of substantial antiquarian studies of buildings, towns and counties which became increasingly popular in the eighteenth century. Profusely illustrated and dedicated to the future king, George II, Dart's publication is clearly not designed to be carried around by anyone visiting the Abbey. Its two substantial volumes were intended to be studied by historians, or to grace the bookshelves of a grand library in a London mansion or country house. The numerous engraved illustrations helped to make the Abbey's monuments familiar to people who might never have visited them in person.

In complete contrast, Thomas Boreman's charming miniature guide is one of a series of *Gigantick Histories* describing the sights of London for children. Other guides covered the Tower of London and St Paul's Cathedral. Very few complete sets of the Westminster Abbey guide have survived and the Abbey's library holds only the first of these three volumes.

2 Funeral effigy of George Monck, 1st Duke of Albemarle, 1670

Monck entered military service at the age of 16 and became a career soldier. During the English civil war he was a commander in the Parliamentary army, and Oliver Cromwell had a high regard for his military expertise. After Cromwell's death, however, Monck was instrumental in negotiating the return of Charles II from exile and the Restoration of the Monarchy in May 1660; for this service he was made Duke of Albemarle by the king. When Monck died, Charles II resolved that he should be buried in the Abbey with all 'the honours and respects imaginable'. The coffin, with the effigy resting on it, lay in state for three weeks in Somerset House before being brought for burial in Henry VII's Lady Chapel, after a magnificent funeral. The effigy's original head and hands were of wax; they have not survived and the present head dates from 1964. The armour may not have been Monck's own as it consists of elements from four different sets, three of which are Dutch. The effigy also originally wore a parliamentary robe and a ducal coronet but these too have been lost. According to an eighteenth-century guidebook, the person who showed visitors the effigies used the coronet to receive the tips that supplemented his 'very inconsiderable' salary. Monck's effigy, like most of the others, was originally set up close to his grave in a standing position. It is displayed here recumbent for the first time since Monck's funeral.

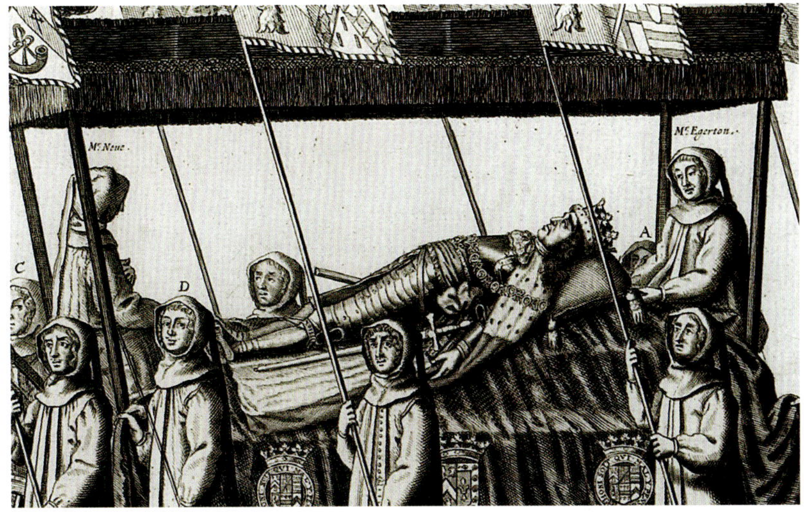

The funeral procession of George Monck, Duke of Albemarle, showing the effigy wearing armour. Engraved by Robert White and collected by Francis Sandford, 1670

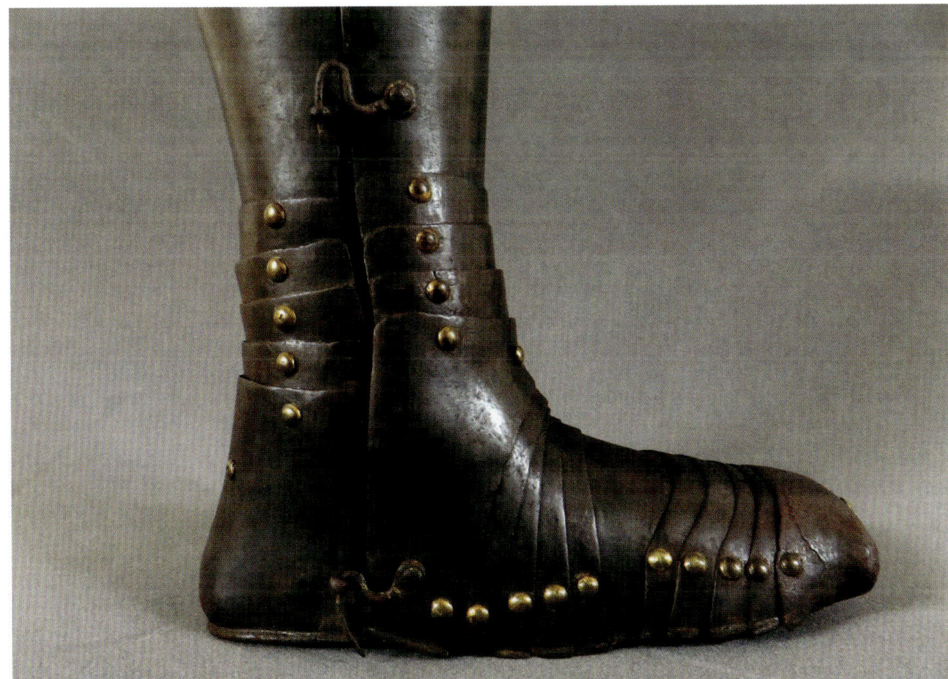

Part of the suit of armour worn by General Monck at his funeral

WA 0867

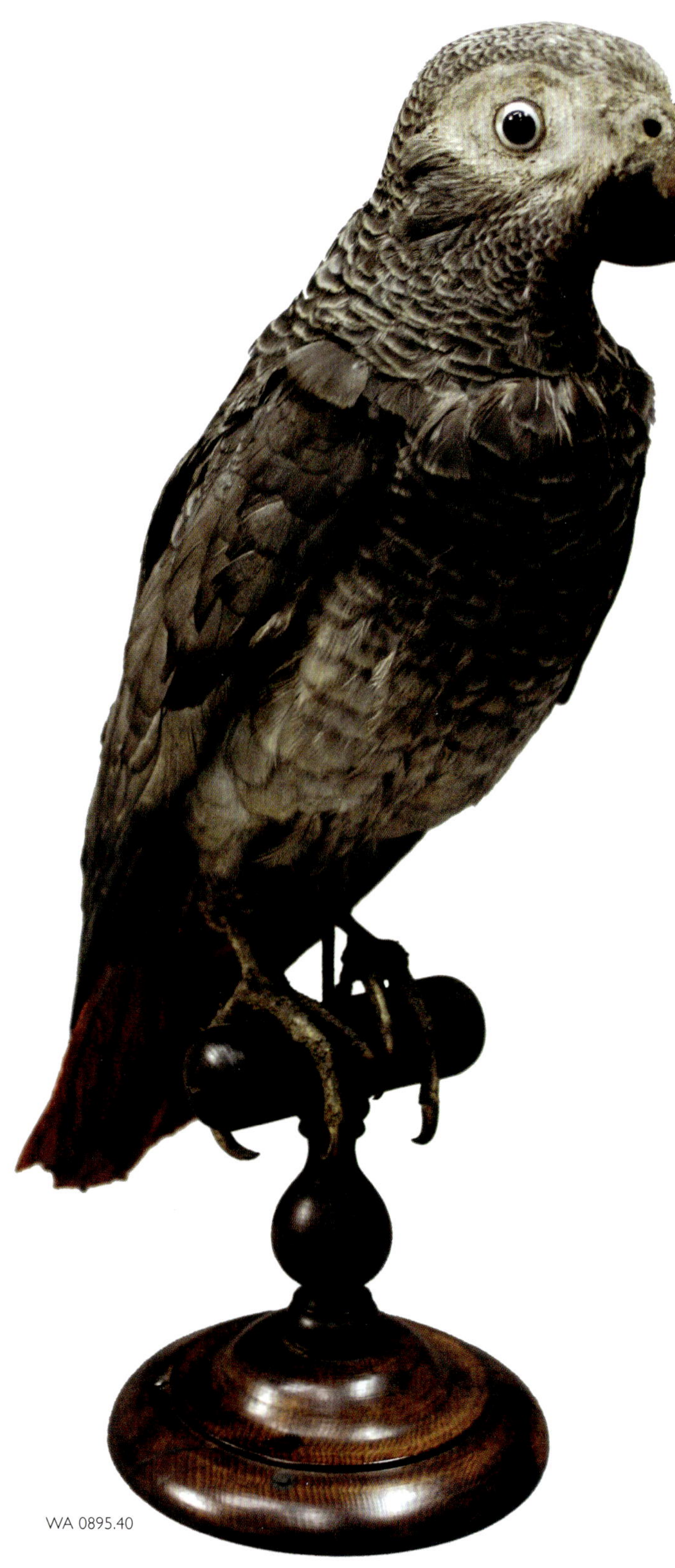

WA 0895.40

3 Parrot belonging to Frances Stuart, Duchess of Richmond and Lennox, 1702

This stuffed mounted parrot is one of the more unusual items in the Abbey's collection. African grey parrots (*Psittacus erithacus*) are known to have been kept as pets in London from the late 1600s onwards, and this one was the companion for 40 years of Frances Stuart, Duchess of Richmond (1647–1702). She was a favourite of Charles II and known as 'La Belle Stuart' on account of her beauty. The parrot died shortly after the duchess and has always been displayed with her effigy, which the duchess had commissioned in her will shortly before her death. It was once thought that the present bird was a later replacement, but X-ray examination has shown that the skeleton, brain and trachea are intact, and that the bird is held together on wire spiked through the body. As this method of taxidermy would not have been used in the late eighteenth or nineteenth centuries, there seems little doubt that this is the original parrot. It is probably the oldest 'stuffed' bird in the UK.

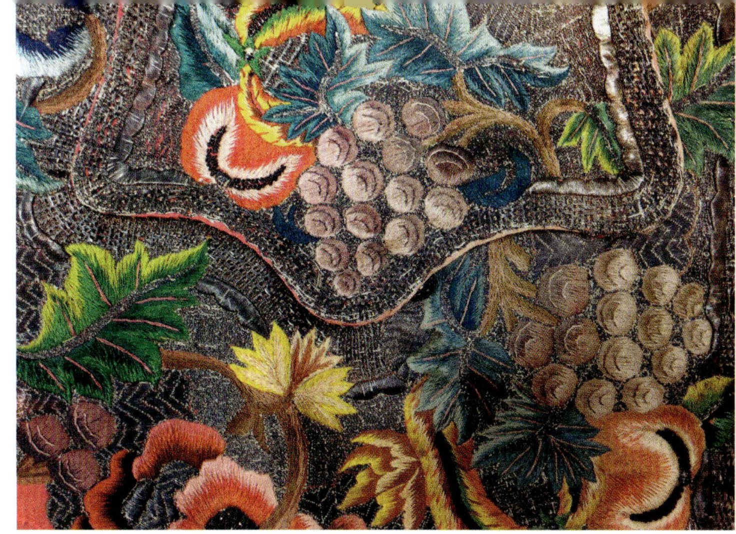

4 Funeral effigy of Edmund Sheffield, 2nd Duke of Buckingham, 1735

This effigy remains exactly as it was carried at the duke's magnificent funeral in January 1736 and is unique in being displayed in its original eighteenth-century case, which is an important survival in its own right. The duke had seen military service in Germany, but was forced to retire to Rome on account of ill health and died there of consumption (tuberculosis) aged only 19. The wax head and hands are so expertly modelled that it seems likely they were cast from the corpse before its return to England. The effigy body is of canvas, stuffed with straw and stiffened with wooden supports. It is dressed in the duke's own clothes, including a waistcoat of pink silk, exquisitely embroidered in coloured threads in a pattern of flowers, bunches of grapes and foliage (above). The velvet and ermine ducal robe was perhaps worn by the duke at the coronation of George II in 1727. The white leather shoes (which are tied on, as the effigy body has no feet) have unfashionably high heels for the date and rest on a roughly carved boar, which is one of the supporters of the Sheffield family coat of arms. A small printed label still inside the wig records that is was made by Francis Caraffa, a 'peruke maker' in Gerrard Street, Soho. A coronet displaying the strawberry-leaf cresting of a duke lies alongside the body.

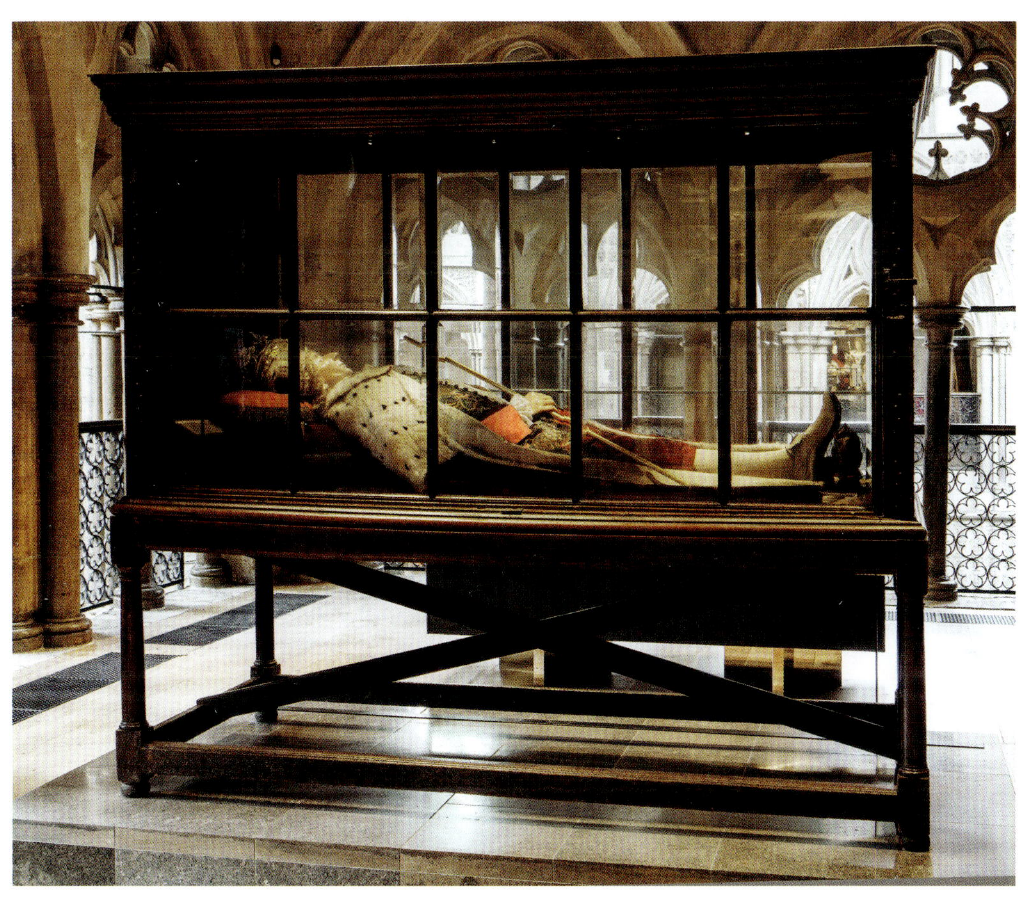

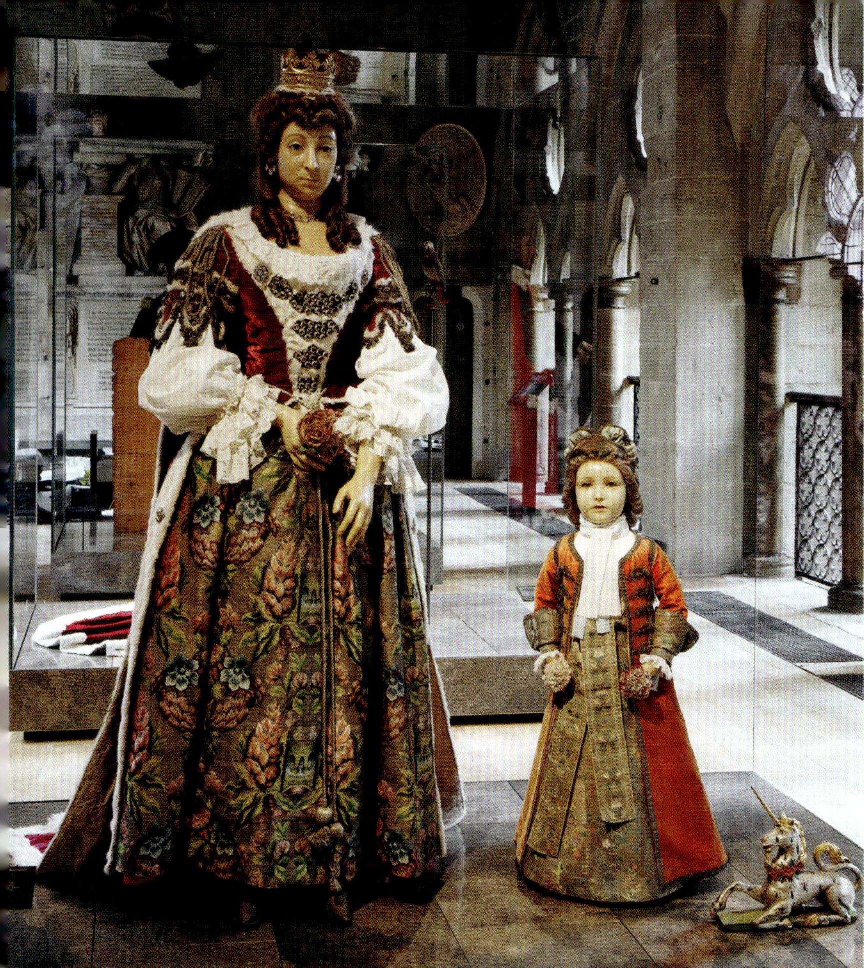

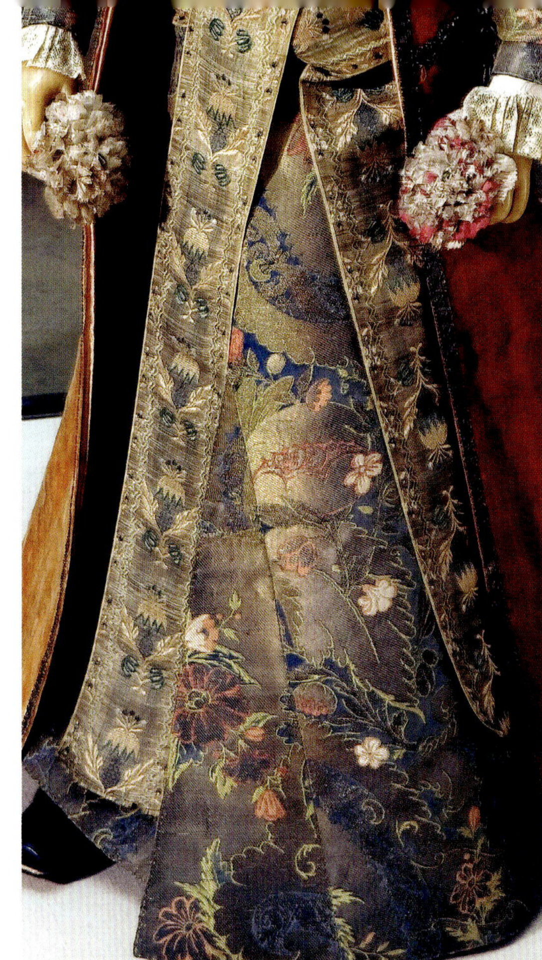

5 Funeral effigies of Catherine Sheffield, Duchess of Buckingham, 1735, and of Robert Sheffield, Marquess of Normanby, 1721 or 1735

Catherine, Duchess of Buckingham, was the illegitimate daughter of James II and so a half-sister of both Queen Mary and Queen Anne. Her effigy was the last to have been carried at a funeral, a contemporary account describing how it was placed under a canopy of state and drawn to the Abbey 'by six horses covered with black velvet'. Unlike earlier effigies, this one was made during the subject's lifetime and dressed under her supervision. The purple robe and the coronet were worn by the duchess for the coronation of George II in 1727. The richly brocaded silk covering the petticoat was woven in France in the late 1730s, while an expensive pair of green silk shoes with buckles (right) are testimony to the wearer's status.

Displayed with the duchess is the poignant effigy of her son Robert, who died in 1715 aged three. He was originally buried in St Margaret's church, beside the Abbey, and it is not certain whether the effigy was made for the funeral or when the boy's remains were transferred to the family vault in the Lady Chapel in 1721. The head and upper body are of wax and the clothes appear to be the boy's own. They include a long floral silk coat and sash (above) beneath a cerise velvet robe. Both garments have slits for leading reins, a reminder of the Marquess's extreme youth. The carved and painted unicorn was a heraldic emblem associated with the boy's mother.

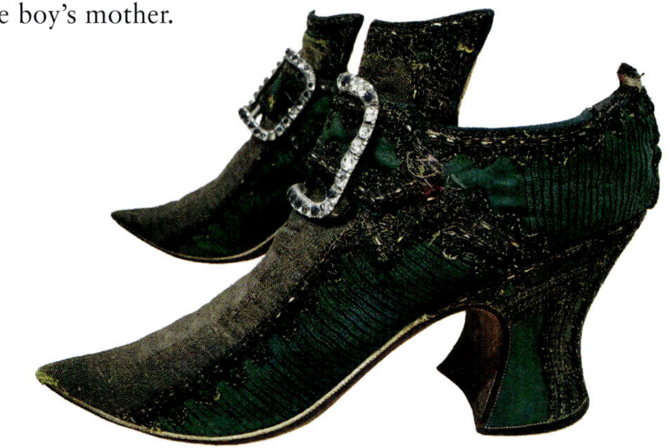

6 Monuments to John Gay, 1736, and Nicholas Rowe, 1742

These monuments are the most significant of the several memorials in the triforium that were originally displayed in the Abbey itself. Dated 1736 and 1742 respectively, they first stood in the south transept, beside the door to St Faith's Chapel (see below). In 1938, after important thirteenth-century wall paintings of St Christopher and St Thomas were found behind them, they were taken up to the triforium, where they remained hidden from public view until the opening of The Queen's Diamond Jubilee Galleries. Both pieces are by the sculptor Michael Rysbrack (1694–1770), whose other works in the Abbey include Sir Isaac Newton's monument (to a design of William Kent) on the north side of the quire screen.

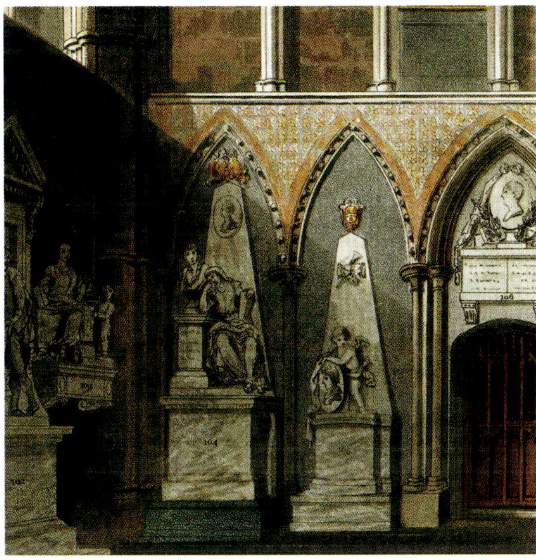

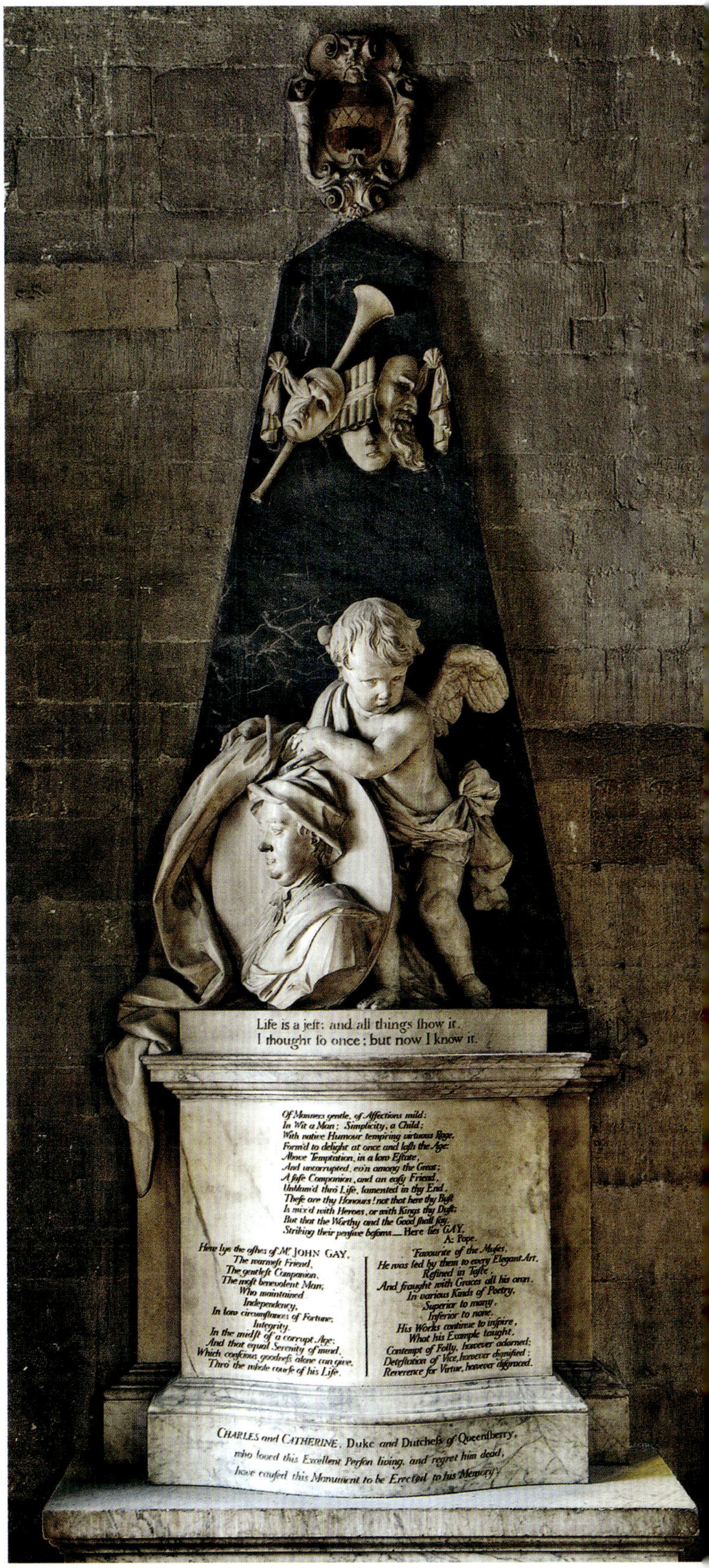

John Gay was a poet and dramatist whose hugely successful *The Beggar's Opera* satirised many well-known personalities of the time, including the prime minister Sir Robert Walpole. Gay's monument (right) shows a *putto* or cherubic infant beside a portrait of the writer. Decorative masks and musical instruments allude to Gay's theatrical career. The poet and playwright Nicholas Rowe, educated at Westminster School, was poet laureate from 1715 and the first modern editor of Shakespeare's plays. His works are now little read, a reminder that the reputations of those buried and commemorated in the Abbey have rarely remained constant. The monument shows a mourning figure leaning against a bust of Rowe. A marble pyramid above displays a portrait of his daughter, Charlotte Fane, whom the monument also commemorates.

7 Effigy of William Pitt, 1st Earl of Chatham, 1778

In the eighteenth century St Paul's Cathedral
increasingly rivalled the Abbey as the place
where significant national figures were buried.
When the politician William Pitt died, the
City of London asked Parliament for him to
be buried in the cathedral but the Abbey was
selected instead, and he was buried in the
north transept. Although the tradition of using
funeral effigies had ended, the gentlemen of the
Abbey choir commissioned an effigy from Mrs
Patience Wright (1725–86), an American wax
modeller who had already modelled Pitt in wax
during his lifetime. She came to the Abbey to
see the existing figures and agreed to provide a
wax bust and hands for 20 guineas. The effigy's
parliamentary robe is not Pitt's own but was
specially made in the space of a week. The new
figure was placed in the Islip Chapel and a
carpenter was employed to fit up an existing
case to accommodate it.

Extraordinary as it now seems, the top of
this case had been made from the Westminster
Retable, the Abbey's medieval altarpiece. That
part of it beneath which Pitt's effigy was to
stand was now painted, causing serious damage
to the retable, which was not rescued from this
ignominious use for several decades. Pitt's effigy
was first put on display in September 1778.
It aroused considerable public interest and, by
doubling the fee for showing the effigy from
threepence to sixpence, the cost of making it
was recouped.

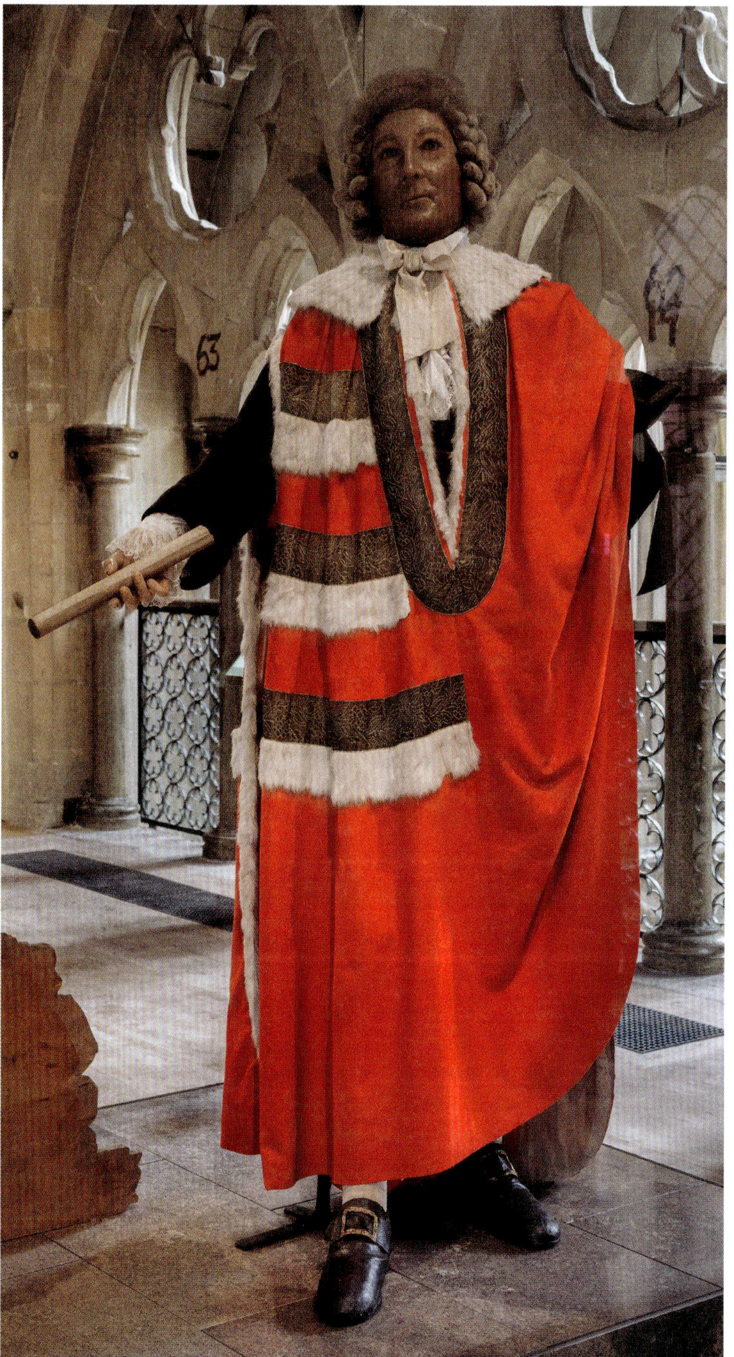

WA 0906

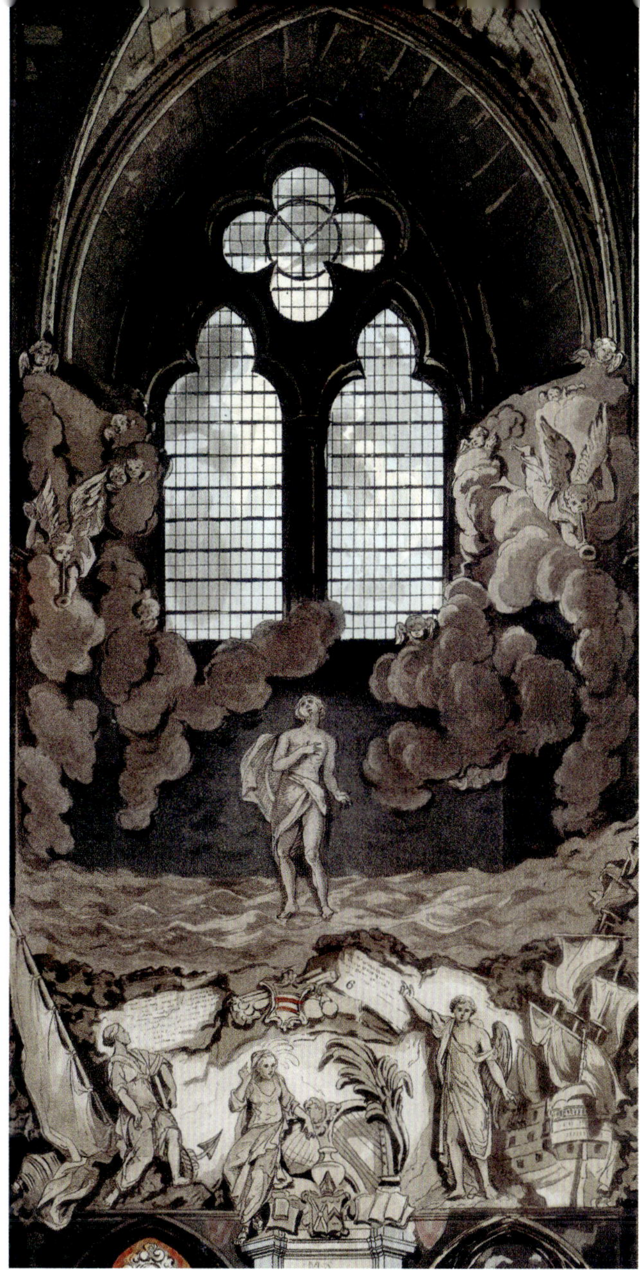

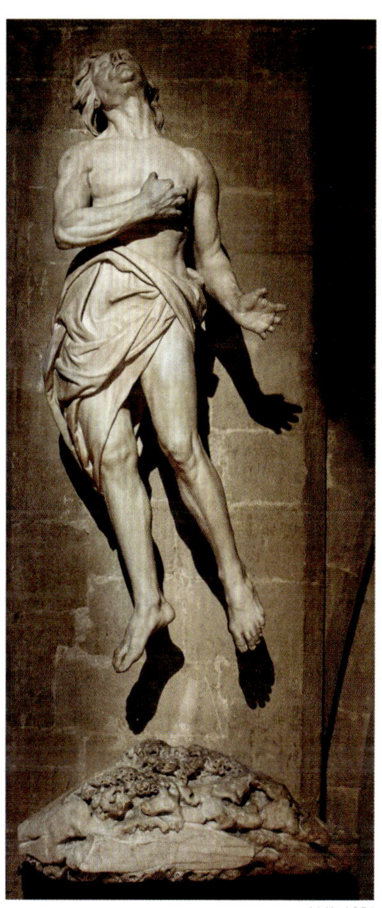

WA 1051

8 Monument to Rear-Admiral Richard Tyrrell, 1770

Visitors to the Galleries quickly notice a marble figure that seems to hang in mid-air and is often assumed to be a religious sculpture. It is in fact a statue of Admiral Richard Tyrrell who spent over twenty years commanding ships in the West Indies and in the process accrued wealth in Jamaica and Antigua derived from the slave trade. He died from a fever in 1766 and was buried at sea, but was subsequently commemorated by a large monument erected around a window in the south side of the Abbey's nave. The work of sculptor Nicholas Read, Tyrrell's figure represented his soul rising from the sea into the clouds of heaven. A skilfully sculpted scene at the base of the window included a depiction of Tyrrell's ship HMS *Buckingham*, alongside maritime imagery and several allegorical figures. In 1882 the monument was greatly curtailed and subsequently new glass was inserted into the window behind it. The lower section alone was retained and of the removed elements, only the figure of Tyrrell himself and one piece of coral have survived. An illustration in Rudolph Ackermann's *Westminster Abbey* (1812) is the only visual record of how the original monument appeared (above left).

9 Effigy of Horatio Nelson, Viscount Nelson, 1806

Nelson's effigy brings the long series of Abbey effigies to its conclusion. He was laid to rest in the crypt of St Paul's Cathedral in January 1806, the profusion of monuments in the Abbey having persuaded Parliament that the Abbey was not appropriate. St Paul's subsequently drew large crowds, who paid a tuppence entrance fee to see the new tomb in the cathedral's crypt. This irritated the Abbey's minor canons and vergers, who traditionally showed the effigies to visitors, and in 1806 they commissioned a rival memorial in the form of a wax effigy to be placed in a case against the west wall of St Andrew's Chapel.

The effigy was the work of Catherine Andras (1775–1860), who was a well-known wax modeller, although her previous works had all been on a much smaller scale. She appears also to have supplied some of the dress and ornaments for the effigy, which may explain why some elements of the costume, such as the vice-admiral's coat, were Nelson's own but others were made specifically for display. The effigy has always had a reputation for being an authentic likeness, even though it mistakenly shows

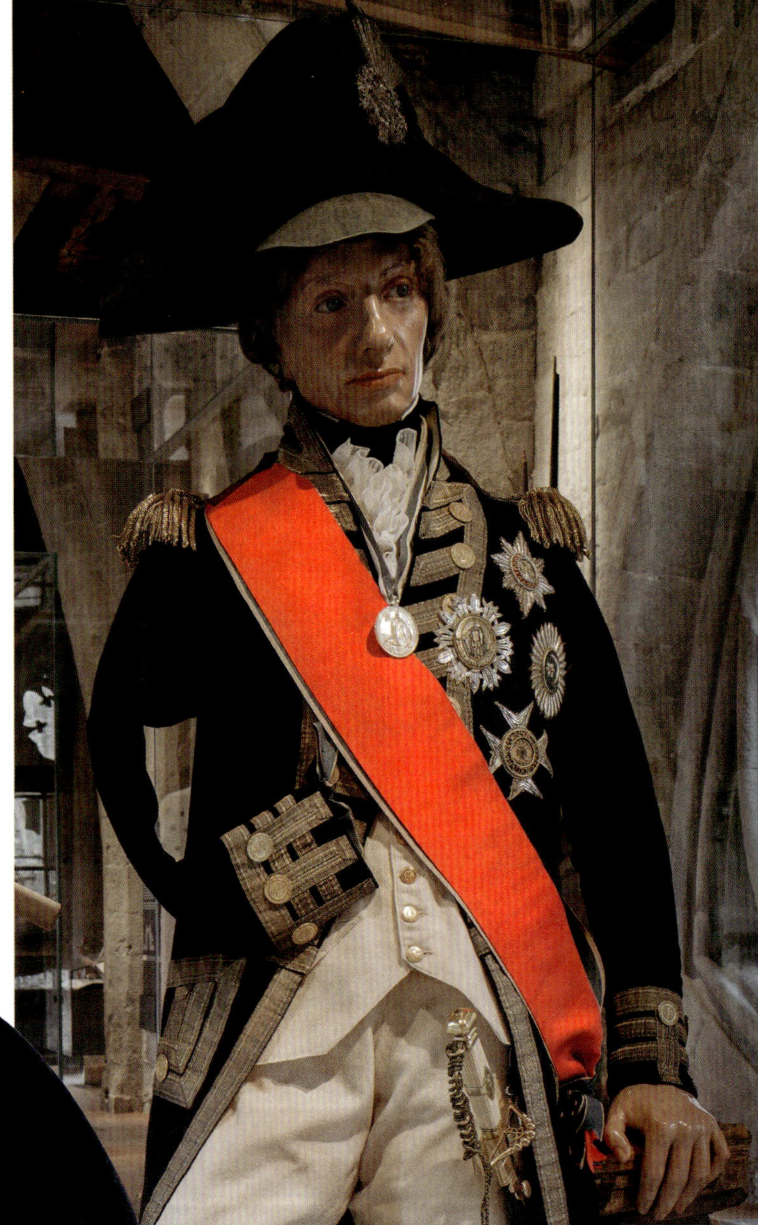

WA 0907

Nelson blind in his left eye rather than his right. In spite of this it is recorded that Emma Hamilton, Nelson's mistress, said the likeness would be perfect 'if a certain lock of hair was disposed in the way his lordship always wore it'. She was permitted to make this alteration.

Sculptors have often used models to develop
their designs. Such models have not always
survived, but the Abbey possesses one or two
that illuminate the process of designing specific
memorials. Louis-Francois Roubiliac's monument
to Lady Elizabeth Nightingale and her husband
Joseph Gascoigne in St Michael's Chapel (right) is
one of the most dramatic in the Abbey. The model
is dated 1758, but the monument was completed in
1761 and consists of a large architectural structure,
from the base of which a skeletal figure of Death
emerges. He aims a dart at Lady Elizabeth, which
her husband attempts in vain to ward off. It is
easy to see how this model (below), which has an
etched scale of 1:15 on the right-hand side, helped
Roubiliac plan his work.

The figure of Arthur Penrhyn Stanley, Dean
of Westminster 1864-81, is of interest for a different
reason, for this model represents a design by Sir
Joseph Boehm which was not in the end carried
out. Seated figures are quite unusual among the

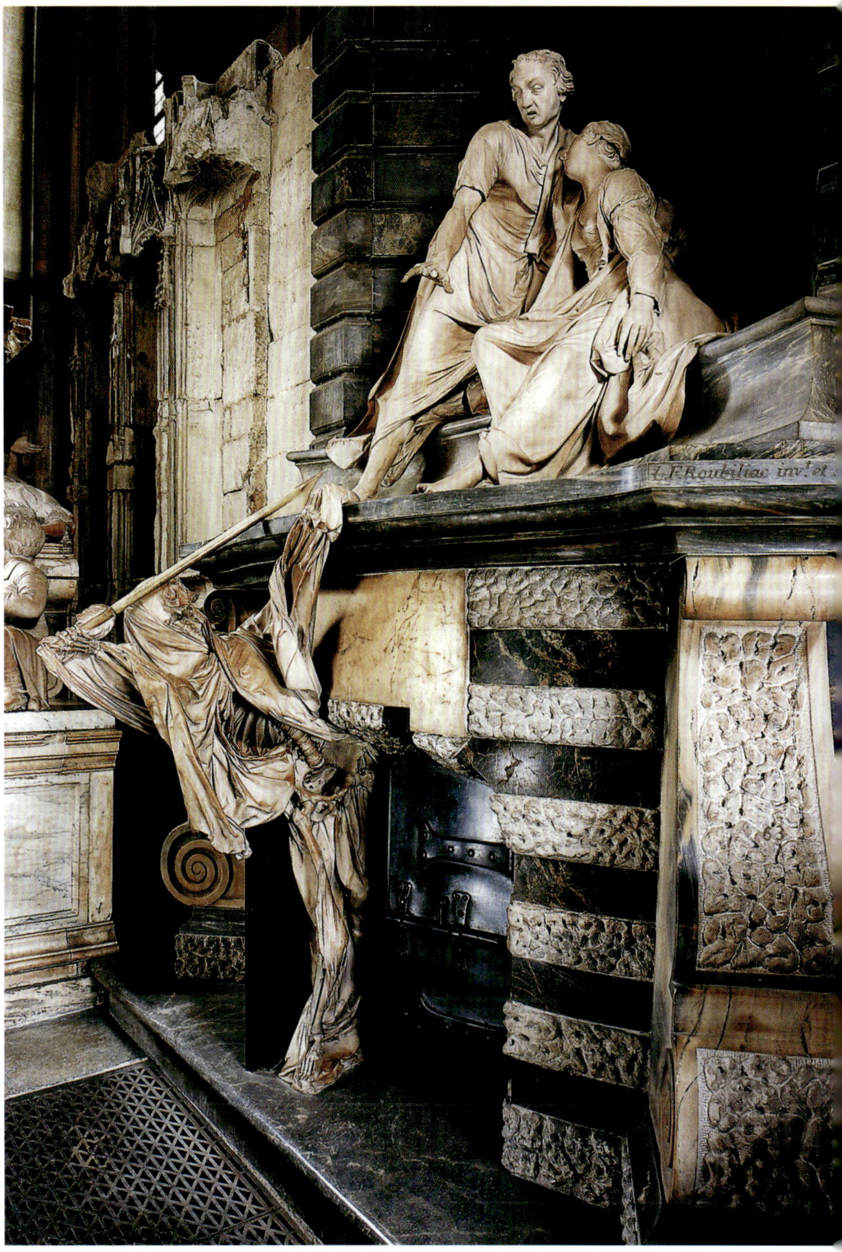

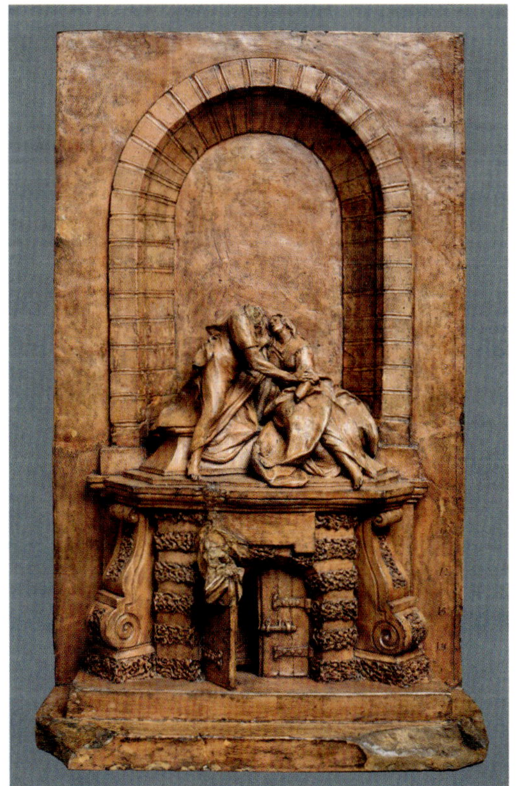

WA 3034

Abbey's monuments, although the design has
echoes of the memorial to the poet William
Wordsworth (installed 1854). The model is worked
to a high standard, and it is not known whether it
was the sculptor himself or the Abbey that rejected
this approach. Whatever the reason, Boehm
abandoned the idea of a memorial showing Stanley
in life in favour of a more traditional chest tomb
with reclining effigy, a style that may have been
thought more appropriate given the monument's
location in Henry VII's Lady Chapel.

The Garfield Weston Foundation
The American Fund for
    Westminster Abbey
The Manton Foundation
The Lord & Lady Harris
The Linbury Trust
The Stoneygate Trust
The Wolfson Foundation
Michael & Melanie Sherwood
David & Claudia Harding
The Dorfman Foundation
The Sackler Trust
John & Catherine Armitage
The Rothschild Foundation
Bank of America
William R. Miller
The Dr Mortimer & Theresa Sackler
    Foundation
Tim Ashley & John Booth
The Allard Family
Sir Harry & Lady Djanogly
The Mercers' Company
The Goldsmiths' Company
The Hintze Family Charitable
    Foundation
The Hobson Charity
Jack & Barbara Bovender
Drs Philip & Jennifer London
Waring & Carmen Partridge
Ronald & Helen Freeman
Natalie Pray
Sir Siegmund Warburg's Voluntary
    Settlement
The Hon. Charles Harris
Stephen Gordon Catto
    Charitable Trust
Gary D. Cohn
Kazie Metzger & John C. Harvey
J. Paul Getty Jr Charitable Trust
The Anton E.B. Schefer Foundation
Okla Basil Meade
Nathan & Marilyn Hayward
Goldman Sachs
Deborah Lehr & John Rogers

CHK Charities
Martin & Zoe Harris
The Sloane Family
Daniel & Anne Ervin
The Hughes-Hallett Family
The Taylor Family Foundation
Golden Bottle Trust
The Frank & William Brake
    Families
Pamela & James Hill
Richard & Amicia Oldfield
Raphaël & Iolanda Kanza
The 29th May 1961 Charitable
    Trust
William & Judith Bollinger
The Lord & Lady Hylton
The Chenevix-Trench Family
Annie Hubbard & Harvey Schwartz
Victor, Carol & The Stewart Family
Stephen & Rebecca Hallman Nacol
Kenneth F. Koen
Peter Stormonth Darling Charitable
    Trust
The Purcell Club
Patrick Higgins
ShareGift
Diane Lokey Farb
The Mosaic Foundation
Jan & Russell MacDonnell
The Charles Hayward Foundation
Jeff & Claudia Blumberg
The Swiftsure Trust
Basil & Maria Postan
Lord Barnby's Foundation
The James Findlay Charitable Trust
The Ruddock Foundation for The
    Arts
The Lord Faringdon Charitable Trust
The Wyfold Charitable Trust
The Stephen & Margaret Gill
    Foundation
The Royal Oak Foundation
High Commission of Canada
The Drapers' Charitable Trust

Emmanuel Roman
Guy Dawson
The Lord & Lady Lupton
Stevenson Family's Charitable Trust
The de Brye Charitable Trust
The Kilfinan Trust
The Peter Cundill Foundation
The Lennox Hannay Charitable Trust
The Lennox & Wyfold Foundation
Joan O'Meara Winant
The Thomas Charitable Foundation
William C. & Susan F. Morris
The George Family Foundation
The Matheson Todd Trust
The Worshipful Company of Masons
Sir Francis & The Hon. Lady Brooke
Sir John Ritblat Family Foundation

UK Campaign Development Board
Guy Weston, Chairman
Will Adderley
Catherine Armitage
Lady Sarah Chatto
Ronald Freeman
The Very Revd Dr John Hall
Lord Harris of Peckham
Valerie Humphrey
Sir Stephen Lamport
John O'Brien
The Marquess of Salisbury
Michael Sherwood
Canon David Stanton

*American Fund for Westminster
    Abbey Appeal Board*
William R. Miller, Chairman
Jack Bovender
June Briggs
Sir David Cannadine
Nathan Hayward
Kazie Metzger
Waring Partridge
Natalie Pray
Victor Stewart